# Brain Quest

Dear Parent,

"It's Fun to Be Smart!" That's not just our slogan, it's our philosophy. For fifteen years we've been adding a big dose of "fun" into learning—first with our bestselling Q&A Brain Quest card decks; then with all the licensed games and products bearing the Brain Quest brand; and now with Brain Quest Workbooks.

At Brain Quest we believe:

- All kids are smart—though they learn at their own speed

- All kids learn best when they're having fun

- All kids deserve the chance to reach their potential—given the tools they need, there's no limit to how far they can go!

BRAIN QUEST WORKBOOKS are the perfect tools to help children get a leg up in all areas of curriculum; they can hone their reading skills or dig in with math drills, review the basics or get a preview of lessons to come. These are not textbooks, but rather true workbooks—best used as supplements to what kids are learning in school, reinforcing curricular concepts while encouraging creative problem solving and higher-level thinking. You and your child can tackle a page or two a day—or an entire chapter over the course of a long holiday break. Your child will be getting great help with basic schoolwork, and you will be better able to gauge how well he or she is understanding course material.

Each BRAIN QUEST WORKBOOK has been written in consultation with an award-winning teacher specializing in that grade, and is compliant with most school curricula across the country. We cover the core competencies of reading, writing, and math in depth—with chapters on science, social studies, and other popular units rounding out the curriculum. Easy-to-navigate pages with color-coded tabs help identify chapters, while Brain Boxes offer parent-friendly explanations of key concepts and study units. That means parents can use the workbooks in conjunction with what their children are learning in school, or to explain material in ways that are consistent with current teaching strategies. In either case, the workbooks create an important bridge to the classroom, an effective tool for parents, homeschoolers, tutors, and teachers alike.

BRAIN QUEST WORKBOOKS all come with a variety of fun extras: a pull-out poster; Brain Quest "mini-cards" based on the bestselling Brain Quest game; two pages of stickers and a Brainiac Award Certificate to celebrate successful completion of the workbook.

Learning is an adventure—a quest for knowledge. At Brain Quest we strive to guide children on that quest, to keep them motivated and curious, and to give them the confidence they need to do well in school . . . and beyond. We're confident that BRAIN QUEST WORKBOOKS will play an integral role in your child's adventure. So let the learning—and the fun—begin!

—The editors of Brain Quest

 This book belongs to:

_____

WORKMAN, BRAIN QUEST, and IT'S FUN TO BE SMART! are registered trademarks of Workman Publishing Co., Inc.

Library of Congress Cataloging-in-Publication Data is available.

ISBN 978-0-7611-4915-6

Workbook series design by Raquel Jaramillo
Illustrations by Kimble Mead

Workman books are available at special discounts when purchased in bulk for premiums and sales promotions as well as for fund-raising or educational use. Special editions or book excerpts also can be created to specification. For details, contact the Special Sales Director at the address below or send an email to specialmarkets@workman.com.

Workman Publishing Co., Inc.
225 Varick Street
New York, NY 10014-4381
workman.com

Printed in the United States of America
First printing June 2008

35 34 33

# Brain Quest
## Grade ②
## Workbook

Written by Liane Onish
Consulting Editor: Jill Swann

WORKMAN PUBLISHING

NEW YORK

# 4

# Contents

5

# Phonics

# Beginning Letters

Say the word for each picture.
What **beginning sound** do you hear?
Write the letter.

**d** og

__ eaf

__ ap

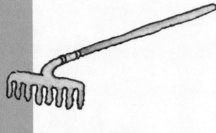

__ ake

__ arrot

__ an

__ est

__ ix

__ ar

__ ear

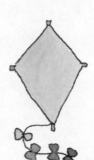

__ ite

__ ie

# Ending Letters

Say the word for each picture.
What **ending sound** do you hear?
Write the letter.

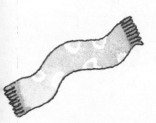   

scar __     fro __     cu __     doo __

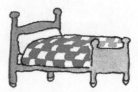  

sea __          ca __          su __

be __          eigh __          bu __

These words end in **ss** or **ll.** What ending sound do
you hear? Write the two letters.

be __ __          dre __ __          do __ __

# It Takes Two

Say the word for each picture.

What beginning sound do you hear?

Find the correct **blend** in the box. Write it on the line.

| bl | br | cl | cr |
|----|----|----|----|
| dr | fl | fr | gl |
| gr | pl | pr | sc |
| sl | sk | sm | sp |
|    | st | sw | tr |

p r esent

__ __ ippers

__ __ oon

__ __ apes

__ __ amp

__ __ uck

# Brain Box

__ __ ing

__ __ ower

__ __ um

**Blends** are two consonants that go together. You can hear both letters in a blend.

Example: **plate**

The blend in this word is **p-l**. When you say **plate**, you can hear both the **p** and **l** sound.

_ _ ee

_ _ is

_ _ asses

_ _ ead

_ _ ool

_ _ oke

_ _ ab

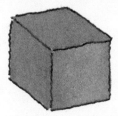

_ _ ock

_ _ ale

_ _ og

_ _ ant

_ _ ock

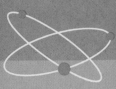

# Shh! Sounds

| ch | sh |
|----|-----|
| th | wh |

Complete each word with a **digraph** from the box.

Draw a line from the word to its picture.

**Phonics**

Digraphs

<u>w h</u> eel

\_\_ \_\_ ark

ben \_\_ \_\_

too \_\_ \_\_

\_\_ \_\_ istle

fi \_\_ \_\_

\_\_ \_\_ eese

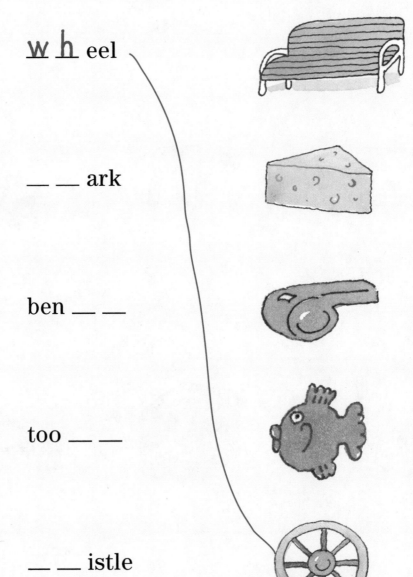

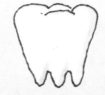

# Brain Box

**Digraphs** are two consonants that are next to each other. Together, they make a new sound.

Example: **thirty**

The **digraph** in this word is **t-h**. When you say **thirty** you don't hear the **t** and **h** sounds separately. You hear the new **th** sound.

# It Takes Three

Say the word for each picture.
Complete each word with a
**consonant cluster** from the box.

| scr | squ |
|-----|-----|
| str | spr |
|     | thr |

<u>s t r</u> awberry

_ _ _ ee

_ _ _ eet

_ _ _ irrel

_ _ _ ub

_ _ _ inkler

_ _ _ ong

_ _ _ one

_ _ _ ay

_ _ _ are

_ _ _ ew

_ _ _ ead

Brain Quest Second Grade Workbook

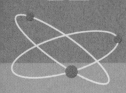
# Lost Letters

Complete each word with a **consonant cluster** from the box.
Draw a line from the word to its picture.

| st | nk |
|----|----|
| mp | lt |
| nd |    |

ba <u>n</u> <u>k</u>

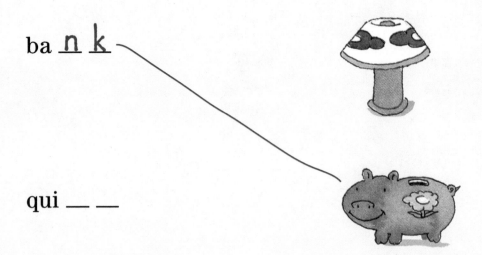

qui __ __

ha __ __

la __ __

toa __ __

sku __ __

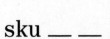

# Brain Box

A **consonant cluster** is a
group of consonants that
are next to each other in
a word.

Example: **land**

The **consonant cluster** in
this word is **n-d.**

Complete each word with a
**consonant cluster** from the box.

Draw a line from the word to its picture.

| rd | rk |
|----|----|
| sk | nt |

pa __ __

te __ __

fo __ __

ma __ __

bi __ __

boa __ __ game

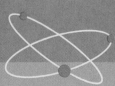
**Phonics**

Hard c and
soft c

# Kite and Circle

Look at the **c** words in the Word Box.

If the word has a **hard c** sound, like **kite,**
write the word next to the kite.

If the word has a **soft c** sound, like **circle,**
write the word next to the circle.

<u>come</u>

_____

_____

_____

kite

| come | cent |
|------|------|
| count | care |
| cellar | card |
| city | cereal |

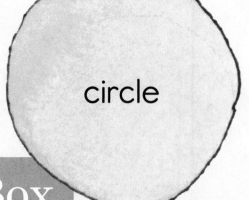

circle

_____

_____

_____

_____

## Brain Box

The letter **c** has two
sounds: a **hard c** sound,
as in **cat**, and a **soft c**
sound, as in **cell.**

# Goose and Jacket

Look at the **g** words in the Word Box.

If the word has a **hard g** sound, like **goose,** write the word next to the goose.

If the word has a **soft g** sound, like **jacket,** write the word next to the jacket.

giraffe

_____

_____

_____

jacket

| game | goat |
|------|------|
| giraffe | gem |
| give | giant |
| genius | grow |

goose

_____

_____

_____

## Brain Box

The letter **g** has two sounds: a **hard g**, as in **grape**, and a **soft g**, as in **gentle.**

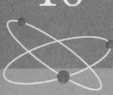

# Picture Cards

Complete each word with a **short vowel**.

### short **a** words

c <u>a</u> t          m __ n

h __ m          __ nt

m __ d          b __ t

### short **e** words

d __ sk          b __ ll

sl __ d          b __ d

h __ n          p __ n

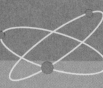

## short i words

f __ sh          w __ g

f __ ll          p __ g

l __ d          h __ d

## short o words

d __ ll          h __ p

r __ ck          f __ x

n __ t          p __ t

## short u words

pl __ m          m __ d

c __ p          b __ s

s __ n          f __ n

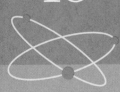
# Short Vowel Sort

Read the words in the Word Boxes.
Write each word next to the picture that has the same **short vowel** sound.

| hat | map | big | got | dad |
|-----|-----|-----|-----|-----|
| box | red | hug | miss | let |

**short a** words

hat

hat

_____

_____

_____

_____

**short e** words

chest

| must | pet | mom | up | ran |
|------|-----|-----|-----|-----|
| ten | top | rush | him | fix |

_____

_____

_____

_____

**short i** words

milk

**short o** words

socks

_____

_____

_____

_____

_____

**short u** words

umbrella

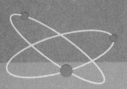

# Ray Takes the Train

Write **ai** or **ay** to complete the **long a** words.

Ray wakes up to the sound of a bluej a y .

He eats cereal on his breakfast tr __ __ .

He takes the tr __ __ n

to the beach.

At the beach, Ray puts shells in his p __ __ l.

Ray loves to pl __ __ in the water.

He watches a beautiful s __ __ lboat

float by.

# Brain Box

"Wow!" he says. "What a

great d __ __ !"

These letter combinations
can make a **long a** sound:
**ai** as in **rain,** and **ay** as in **ray.**

# What Do You See?

Write **e, ea, ee,** or **ey** to complete the **long e** words.

My dad is driving us to the  b __ __ ch.

Words with the
**long e** sound:
**e, ea, ee, ey**

There are  thr __ __  of us in the car.

On the way w __  pass a tr __ __ .

There are lots of  b __ __ s  in the  tr __ __ .

They are making  hon __ __ .

## Brain Box

Luckily, the bees don't sting  m __ !

These letter combinations
can make a **long e** sound:
**ee** as in **wheel, ea** as in
**flea,** and **ey** as in **money.**

Finally we reach the  s __ __ !

Sometimes, the letter **e** all
by itself can also make a
**long e** sound, as in **he.**

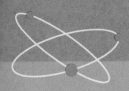

# I Love Riddles!

Write **i, ie, igh,** or **y** to complete the **long i** words.

**Phonics**

Words with the
**long i** sound:
**i, ie, igh, y**

I am not a baby. I am not an adult.

I am a ch __ ld.

I help you see in the dark.

I am a flashl __ __ __ t.

Wear me around your neck.

I am a t __ __ .

I buzz in your ears. I am a fl __ .

Long ago, I wore a suit of armor.

I am a kn __ __ __ t.

You can't keep a secret from

# Brain Box

us! We are sp __ __ s.

These letters can make
a **long i** sound: **y** as in **by**
and **igh** as in **high.**

Sometimes these letters
can also make a **long i**
sound: **i** as in **find** and **ie**
as in **pie.**

You have to peel me.

I am an orange r __ nd.

# Let's Roll Along

Write **oa, ow,** or **o** to complete the **long o** words.

**Phonics**

Words with the **long o** sound:
**oa, ow, o**

sailb __ __ t

t __ __ d

g __

g __ __ t

c __ ld

r __ __ d

sn __ __

## Brain Box

These letter combinations can make a **long o** sound: **oa** as in **float** and **ow** as in **low.**

Sometimes, the letter **o** all by itself can also make a **long o** sound, as in **no.**

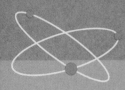

# A Few Clues

Write **u, ew, ue,** or **ui** to complete the **long u** words.

Words with the
**long u** sound:
**u, ew, ue, ui**

I am the color of the sky.

I am bl __ __ .

I can be an apple, an orange, or a grape.

I am fr __ __ t.

You can dance to me.

I am m __ sic.

The candle was still burning.

The man bl __ __ it out.

I stick things together.

I am gl __ __ .

## Brain Box

These letter combinations make the
**long u** sound: **ue** as in **due**, **ui** as in
**juice,** and **ew** as in **flew.**

Sometimes the letter **u** all by itself
can also make a **long u** sound, as in
**unicorn.**

I am a toy that's still in the box.

I am brand-n __ __ .

# Vote for E!

Add an **e** to the end of these **short vowel** words to make new **long vowel** words.

can      can <u>e</u>

man      man __

cap      cap __

cub      cub __

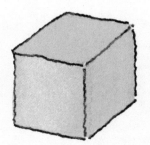

tub      tub __

## Brain Box

A **short vowel** can become a **long vowel** when you add an **e** to the end of some words.

| Example: **kit** + **e** = **kite** |

When you add an **e** to the end of **kit**, you get **kite**. **Kite** has a **long i** sound.

pin      pin __

# Mix-Ups

Unscramble each word.
Write the correct word on the line.

e s i m l      __smile__

a t e g      _____

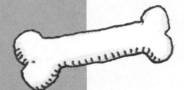

n b e o      _____

b e c u      _____

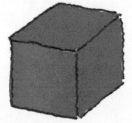

p r e o      _____

i e m d      _____

z m e a      _____

n n e i      _____

Phonics

Final e

# Bears and Squares

Write **air, are,** or **ear** to complete the words below the honey jars.

h <u>a r e</u>

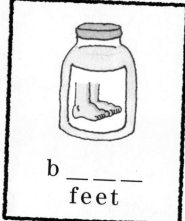

p _ _ _

b _ _ _ _
feet

c h _ _ _ _

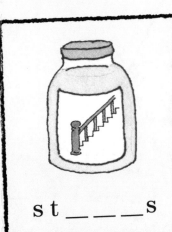

s t _ _ _ s

b _ _ _ _

## Brain Box

The letter combinations **are, ear,** and **air** can have the same sound. For example, **fair, wear,** and **care.**

# Girl with Curls

Write **er, ir,** or **ur** to complete the words.

c __ __ tain

g i r l

c __ __ ls

sh __ __ t

f __ __ n

wat __ __

sk __ __ t

## Brain Box

The letter combinations
**er, ir,** and **ur** all have the
same sound. For example,
**bird, hurt,** and **father.**

# Clark's Chores

Write **ar, or, ore,** or **our** to complete the words.

Cl __ __ k lives on a f __ __ m.

Today, he has ch __ __ __ s to do.

First, Cl __ __ k feeds the h __ __ se.

He puts hay in the b __ __ n.

He sweeps the p __ __ ch.

He p __ __ __ s milk for the cat.

Then, Cl __ __ k waters the vegetable g __ __ den.

He makes a list of things he needs from the

st __ __ __ .

He picks f __ __ __ ears of c __ __ n for dinner.

# Joy and Her Hound Dog

Write **oi, oy** or **ou, ow** to complete the word below the pictures.

Then sort the words by sound on the cards.

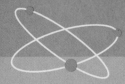

Phonics

Diphthongs:
**oi** and **oy**;
**ou** and **ow**

cl <u>o</u> <u>w</u> n

b __ __

c __ __ n

s __ __ l

c __ __

m __ __ se

t __ __

h __ __ se

**oi, oy**

_____

_____

_____

**ou, ow**

clown

_____

_____

_____

_____

# Brain Box

**Diphthongs** are two vowels that go together to make a new sound.

Example: **oi** as in **noise** and **oy** as in **joy.**

Both of these **diphthongs** make the same sound.

# The Cook in the Moon

Read the words in the Word Box.

Write the words that have the same vowel sound as **cook** next to the cook.

Write the words that have the same vowel sound as **moon** next to the moon.

Phonics

**Short** and **long oo** sounds

_____

_____

_____

_____

cook

| broom | book | food | good |
|-------|------|------|------|
| look | noodle | spoon | wood |

__broom__

_____

_____

moon

_____

## Brain Box

Sometimes the same letter combinations have different sounds. Two **o**s together can have a **long oo** sound, as in **moon**, or a **short oo** sound, as in **cook**.

Brain Quest Second Grade Workbook

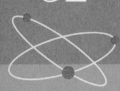

**32**

# Rhyme Time!

Write **al, all, aw,** or **o** to complete each rhyme.

**Phonics**

Variant vowel
sounds:
**al, all, aw, o**

b <u>a l l</u> on the w <u>a l l</u>

w __ __ k  and  t __ __ k

m __ th  in the  br __ th

str __ __  on  a  sees __ __

l __ ng  s __ ng

cr __ __ l  and  b __ __ l

Brain Quest Second Grade Workbook

# Spelling and Vocabulary

# Sort the Shorts

Sort the words in the Word Box by vowel sound.
Write the words on the correct vowel card.

| jet | bath | vest | chick | rod |
|-----|------|------|-------|-----|
| ink | bus | tag | skunk | sock |
| rat | spot | neck | luck | mitt |

**Spelling and Vocabulary**

Short vowel review

### short **a**

bath

_____

_____

### short **e**

_____

_____

_____

### short **i**

_____

_____

_____

### short **o**

_____

_____

_____

### short **u**

_____

_____

_____

# Brain Box

Look at these **short vowel** words:
**hat, bed, rig, rod,** and **cup.** They all
have the same spelling patterns:

consonant / short vowel / consonant.

You can use this pattern to help you
spell similar words.

Answer the riddles with words from the Word Box.

A pen is filled with me. I help you write.

I am i n k .

I am a baby bird. I am a __ __ __ __ __ .

I fly high in the sky. I am a __ __ __ .

I am yellow and take you to school.

I am a __ __ __ .

I am black and white and very smelly.

I am a __ __ __ __ __ .

You use me to fish. I am a fishing __ __ __ .

I keep your foot warm and clean.

I am a __ __ __ __ .

You look at me when you want to know the price.

I am a price __ __ __ .

You take me when you get dirty.

I am a __ __ __ __ .

# Crossword Craze

Complete the long vowel words with a **vowel** and a **final e.**
Write the words in the puzzle.

## Across

2. She a t e the apple.

4. We have a flat t __ r __ .

5. A tree with needles: p __ n __ .

6. Our whole family gets together on New Year's __ v __ .

8. Four plus five equals n __ n __ .

9. A raisin is a dried gr __ p __ .

## Down

1. A 3-D map of the world is a g l __ b __ .

3. Those are hers, th __ s __ are mine.

4. Another word for "melody": t __ n __ .

7. Tomatoes grow on a v __ n __ .

9. They g __ v __ the money they collected to charity.

10. Every Sunday I talk to my grandma on the ph __ n __ .

**1** ⬜⬜⬜⬜

**2** | a | **3** t | e |

**9** ⬜⬜⬜ **10** ⬜

**4** ⬜⬜⬜⬜

**5** ⬜⬜⬜⬜ **6** ⬜ **7** ⬜⬜

**8** ⬜⬜⬜⬜

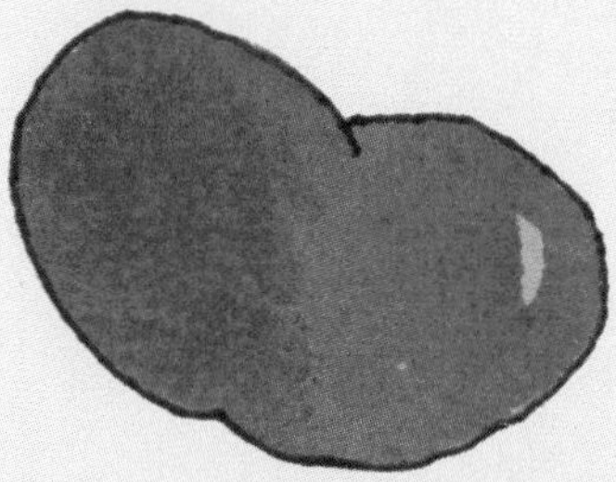

# Long a Words

Complete each sentence with a **long a** word from the Word Box.

Artists like to draw and ___paint___.

The bird is in the _____.

My favorite thing to eat is _____.

I asked the postman for the _____.

We rehearsed our parts for the _____.

He fell down, but he is _____.

| okay |
| cake |
| paint |
| cage |
| play |
| mail |

Now sort the **long a** words on the cards below.

a_e
_____
_____

ay
_____
_____

ai
_paint_
_____

# Brain Box

Look for these spelling patterns in **long a** words:
**ai** as in **rain, ay** as in **ray**, and **a_e** as in **page.**

# Long e Words

Complete each sentence with a **long e** word from the Word Box.

My name is _____ .

I don't like to _____ tired so I go to

bed when it's time to _____ .

If I can't fall asleep, I count _____ .

I always have sweet _____ .

In one dream, I swam like a _____

and found a chest full of _____ .

| sheep |
| --- |
| seal |
| money |
| me |
| Joey |
| sleep |
| dreams |
| be |

Dreams make _____ happy!

Now sort the **long e** words on the cards below.

**ee**
_____

**ea**
_____

**ey**
_____
_____

**e**
_____
_____

## Brain Box

Brain Quest Second Grade Workbook

Look for these spelling patterns in **long e** words: **ee** as in **wheel**, **ea** as in **flea**, **ey** as in **money**, and **e** as in **he**.

# Long i Words

Complete each sentence with a **long i** word from the Word Box.

| |
|---|
| fries |
| white |
| right |
| blind |
| lie |
| bite |
| night |
| dry |

I love eating french _____ .

My dog does not _____ .

The opposite of day is _____ .

Someone who can't see is _____ .

The opposite of wrong is _____ .

A zebra is black and _____ .

I tell the truth. I don't _____ .

The opposite of wet is _____ .

# Brain Box

Look for these spelling patterns in **long i** words: **y** as in **by**, **igh** as in **high**, **i** as in **find**, **ie** as in **pie**, and **i_e** as in **kite**.

Now sort the **long i** words on the cards below.

y

igh

i

ie

i_e

# Long o Words

Complete each sentence with a
**long o** word from the Word Box.

At the end of the _____ there is a pot

of _____ .

I _____ a letter to a friend at camp.

I eat _____ with butter for breakfast.

My mom always puts a

_____ in my lunch box.

| toast | go |
| wrote | gold |
| rainbow | grow |
| throat | note |

The opposite of stop is _____ .

I'm sick. I have a sore _____ .

Every day I _____ bigger.

Now sort the **long o** words on the
cards below.

## Brain Box

Look for these spelling
patterns in **long o** words:
**oa** as in **float**, **ow** as in
**low**, **o** as in **no**, and **o_e**
as in **rode**.

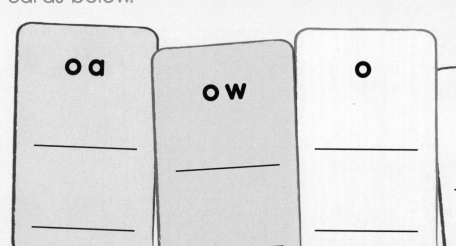

oa

ow

o

o_e

_____

_____

_____

_____

_____

_____

_____

_____

# Long u Words

Complete each sentence with a **long u** word from the Word Box.

| |
|---|
| unicorn |
| juice |
| utensils |
| clue |
| huge |
| flew |
| fruit |
| cute |

A _____ has a horn on its head.

I drink orange _____ .

A detective follows a _____ .

Puppies and kittens are so _____ !

The opposite of tiny is _____ .

A knife and a fork are eating _____ .

The airplane _____ in the sky.

Apples are my favorite _____ .

**Spelling and Vocabulary**

Long u words

# Brain Box

Look for these spelling patterns in **long u** words: **ue** as in **due**, **u** as in **universe**, **ui** as in **cruise**, **ew** as in **blew**, and **u_e** as in **mule**.

Now sort the **long u** words on the cards below.

ue

ew

u

ui

u _ e

# Silent Letters

These words all have **silent letters.**
Say each word out loud as you copy it.
Then circle the silent letter.

comb ___comb___

lamb _____

sign _____

knife _____

kneel _____

sword _____

high _____

write _____

sigh _____

Write a sentence using one of the words above.

_____

_____

# 44

# Compound It!

Use a word from the Word Box to make a **compound word.**
Use the pictures as clues.

pan + _cake_ = _pancake_

air + _____ = _____

bath + _____ = _____

straw + _____ = _____

key + _____ = _____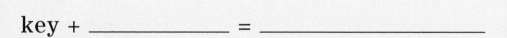

note + _____ = _____

flower + _____ = _____

gold + _____ = _____

**Spelling and Vocabulary**

Compound words

| plane |
| berry |
| book |
| fish |
| pot |
| hole |
| robe |
| cake |

# Brain Box

A **compound word** is a word made up of two smaller words.

Sometimes the meanings of the small words can help you figure out the meaning of the **compound word.**

Brain Quest Second Grade Workbook

Draw a line from each word in column A to a word in column B to make a common **compound word**. Then write the compound word in column C.

## A

back

camp

bag

book

grape

sky

home

bean

bird

snow

## B

cage

bone

pole

work

flakes

line

pipes

fire

case

vine

## C

backbone

# The Why of Y

The words in the Word Box all end in **y,** but they are not all pronounced the same way.

Sort the words by vowel sound.

Write the **y** words with the same sound as **bunny** on the bunny card.

Write the **y** words with the same sound as **spy** on the spy card.

**Spelling and Vocabulary**

Y words with long e and long i sounds

baby

cry

happy

story

fly

mommy

merry

lullaby

my

sky

bunny

spy

Use words from the Word Box to complete the sentence.

A _____ sings a _____

to her _____ .

# A Silly Story

Read the story.
Circle all the words that end in **y.**
Then sort the words on the cards below.

Spelling and
Vocabulary

Y words with
long e and
long i sounds

There once was a (crazy) canary. He lived in the
city. In January, the tiny bird decided to fly to the
country to visit his family. He packed his bag with
a supply of food, a library book, and his favorite
fuzzy pajamas. Then he flew into the sky. After
months of traveling, he finally arrived in July.
Everyone was so happy!

"Now it's time to go home," chirped the pretty
bird.

"But why?" said his father.

"Because I am shy" was his reply.

## y words with **long e** sound

__crazy__    _____

_____    _____

_____    _____

_____    _____

_____    _____

## y words with **long i** sound

_____

_____

_____

_____

_____

_____

_____

_____

_____

# Zara's Yard Sale

Complete the words that have the
same vowel sound as **Zara** and **yard**.

  al a r m clock

  j __ __ of m __ __ bles

  toy c __ __ s

  y __ __ n

  toy f __ __ m

  shin gu __ __ ds

  st __ __ sweater

# Spell Like a Shark!

Write all the **ar** words from the Word Box in alphabetical order.

| start | march | far |
|-------|-------|------|
| party | park | hard |
| cart | garden | harm |
| art | large | bar |

__art_____          _____          _____

_____          _____          _____

_____          _____          _____

_____          _____          _____

Write two sentences using any of the **ar** words in the Word Box.

_____

_____

_____

_____

# All About Fern

Circle all the words that have the same vowel sound as **Fern.**

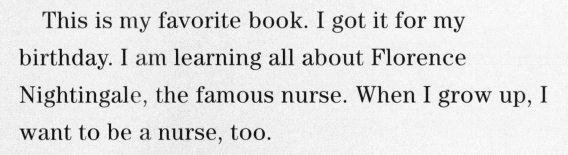

My name is Fern, and I am the third tallest girl in my class. I am also the only person in my class who has curly hair. Can you believe that?

This is my favorite book. I got it for my birthday. I am learning all about Florence Nightingale, the famous nurse. When I grow up, I want to be a nurse, too.

Say each word you circled.
Listen to the vowel sound.
Sort the words by spelling pattern on the **ear, er, ir, ur** cards below.

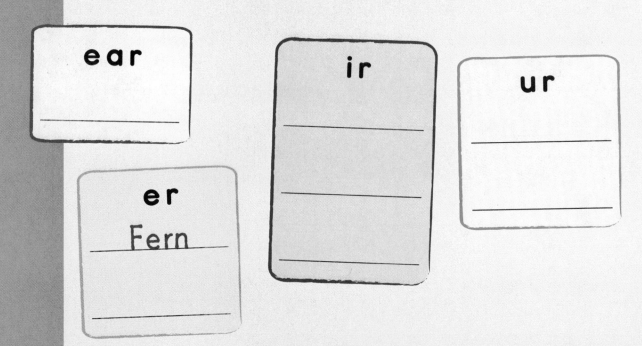

**ear**
_____

**er**
Fern
_____

**ir**
_____
_____
_____

**ur**
_____

# Spell Like a Bird

Say each word in the Word Box.
Sort the words by spelling pattern on the cards below.

| | | | |
|---|---|---|---|
| pearl | lavender | letter | glitter |
| lantern | search | earth | urgent |
| burn | first | purpose | early |
| bird | hurt | chirp | dirty |
| curb | shirt | perfect | earn |

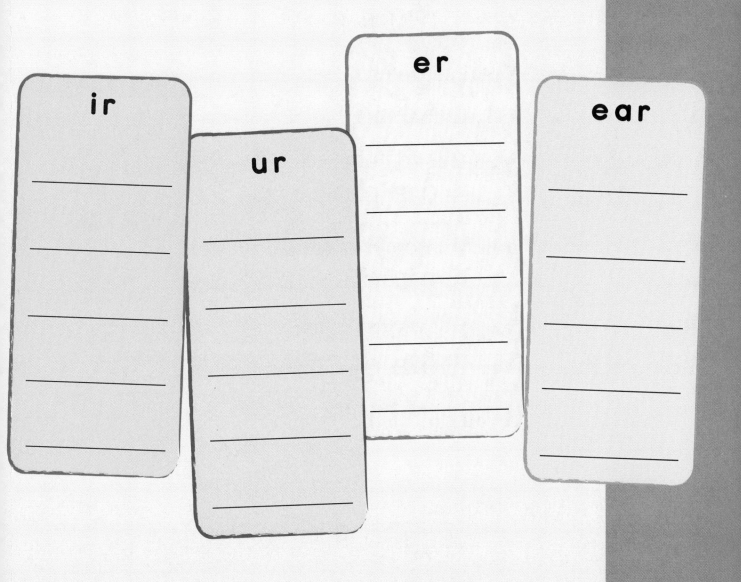

**ir**

**ur**

**er**

**ear**

# Boar Game

Read the clues.
Unscramble the answers.

Do this to get milk from a bottle into a glass.

R P O U  __ __ __ __

Some people make this sound when they sleep.

O N S R E  __ __ __ __ __

Watch out for these on a rosebush.

H T R N O S  __ __ __ __ __ __

This word is the opposite of "less."

O M R E  __ __ __ __

A lion makes this sound.

A R O R  __ __ __ __

You open this to come in.

O R D O  __ __ __ __

This number comes after three.

U R O F  __ __ __ __

This gets covered by a rug.

O R O L F  __ __ __ __ __

A bird can do this in the sky.

R A S O  __ __ __ __

A unicorn has this on his head.

R N O H  __ __ __ __

Sort the words you unscrambled by spelling pattern on the cards below.

**oar**

_____

_____

**oor**

_____

**or**

_____

**ore**

_____

_____

**our**

_____

_____

All the words you sorted are hidden in the word scramble.

Find the words and circle them.

| T | B | T | H | O | U | F | N |
|---|---|---|---|---|---|---|---|
| H | U | F | O | U | R | L | S |
| O | R | S | A | D | O | O | R |
| R | A | N | O | A | U | O | U |
| N | M | O | R | E | R | R | O |
| S | O | R | O | R | B | I | T |
| S | R | E | A | S | O | A | R |
| P | O | U | R | F | O | O | R |

# A Cow in the House!

Complete the clues with words that have the same spelling pattern as **how** and **mouth**. Write the words in the puzzle.

## Across

1. Milk comes from  c __ __ __ .

3. A  h __ __ __ __  is a building where you live.

5. Is your hair the color  br __ __ __ ?

7. What goes up must come  d __ __ __ .

9. A circus  cl __ __ __  makes people laugh.

11. I use a  t __ __ __ __  to get dry.

## Down

2. A tiny animal that likes cheese is a

   m __ __ __ __ .

4. If you lose something, go to the lost and

   f __ __ __ __ .

6. The opposite of "in" is  __ __ __ .

8. The opposite of "later" is  n __ __ .

10. To yell something is to  sh __ __ __ .

12. A king wears a  cr __ __ __  on his head.

13. The opposite of "quiet" is  l __ __ __ .

14. A type of bird that goes hoot is an  o __ __ .

# Roy Points

Sort the words by spelling pattern on the cards below.

| coin | oyster | boil | enjoy |
|------|--------|------|-------|
| boy | noise | royal | choice |
| toy | join | point | annoy |
| voice | oil | loyal | destroy |

**oi**

_____     _____

_____     _____

_____     _____

_____     _____

**oy**

_____     _____

_____     _____

_____     _____

_____     _____

# Moose and Books

All the words in the Word Box are **oo** words, but they are not all pronounced the same way.

Write the **oo** words with the same sound as **moose** on the moose card.

Write the **oo** words with the same sound as **book** on the book card.

| balloon | spoon | foot | look | spooky |
|---------|-------|------|------|--------|
| hood | wood | tooth | shook | loose |

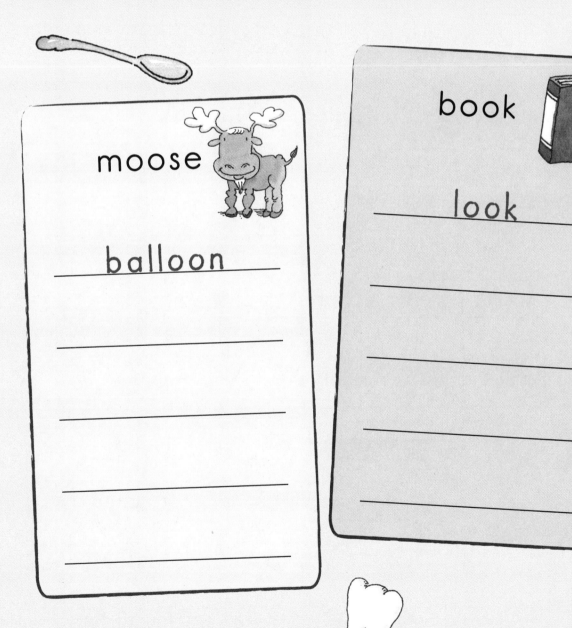

**moose**

balloon

_____

_____

_____

_____

**book**

look

_____

_____

_____

_____

_____

# Opposites!

Read each sentence.
Color the **antonym** of the
underlined word in the sentence.

A great dane is a <u>large</u> dog!

| small | giant | big |

The balloon flew <u>up</u> in the air.

| high | down | left |

She went to the <u>front</u> of the line.

| top | start | back |

It is so <u>hot</u> today!

| warm | cold | rainy |

Draw a line from each word to its **antonym.**

terrible                    dry

before                      thrilled

disappointed                after

soaked                      fabulous

# Brain Box

**Antonyms** are words that
have opposite meanings.

# So Many Snowflakes!

Draw a line from each snowflake to its **synonym**.

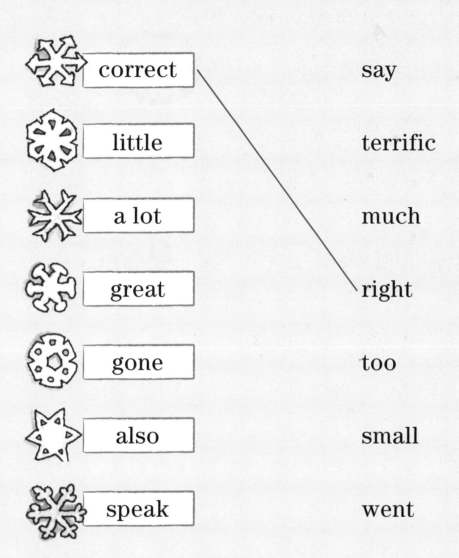

correct — right

little

a lot

great

gone

also

speak

say

terrific

much

right

too

small

went

Fill in the blanks with **synonyms** from the Word Box.

challenging

sparkle

moist

missing

lost _____

shine _____

difficult _____

damp _____

# Brain Box

**Synonyms** are words that have similar meanings.

Brain Quest Second Grade Workbook

# Write It Right

Circle the correct **homophone** in each sentence.

**Spelling and Vocabulary**

Homophones

It is half past the our / hour.

 There is a pair / pear tree in the yard.

 She broke her right / write leg.

 The clouds are hiding the son / sun.

On the lines below, write two sentences for two of the words you did not circle.

_____

_____

_____

_____

# Brain Box

**Homophones** are words that sound the same but have different spellings and meanings.

# Same Sounds

Circle the correct **homophone** in each sentence.

I am going to ballet class, too / two.

Look at that fish's  I / eye!

All the boats are on sale / sail.

The movie is playing for two weaks / weeks only.

On the lines below, write two sentences for two of the words you did not circle.

_____

_____

_____

_____

# More than One

Write the **plural** for each word by adding **s** or **es**.

apple <u>apples</u>     ax _____

glass _____     box _____

cat _____     sandwich _____

fox _____     pen _____

brush _____     crutch _____

watch _____     bus _____

Spelling and Vocabulary

Plurals with s, es

# Brain Box

**Plural** means more than one.

Add **s** to make most nouns plural.

Add **es** if the noun ends in **sh, ch, tch, s,** or **x.**

# Plural Math

Subtract and add letters to spell the **irregular plural** of each word.

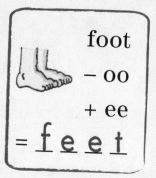

foot
– oo
+ ee
= <u>f</u> <u>e</u> <u>e</u> <u>t</u>

woman
– a
+ e
= _ _ _ _ _

**Spelling and Vocabulary**

Irregular plurals

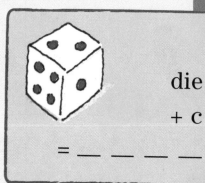

die
+ c
= _ _ _ _

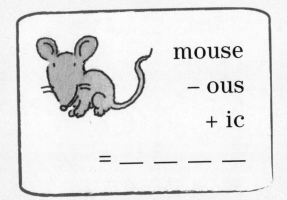

child
+ ren
= _ _ _ _ _ _ _ _

tooth
– oo
+ ee
= _ _ _ _ _

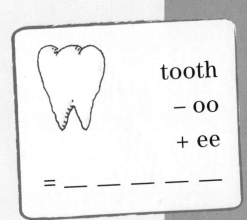

mouse
– ous
+ ic
= _ _ _ _

# Brain Box

Some plurals are **irregular.**

This means you don't add **s** or **es** at the end to make the word plural.

You have to change the whole word.

# Color Search

Circle all the **color words** in the puzzle.

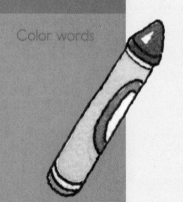

| V | O | R | A | I | G |
|---|---|---|---|---|---|
| I | R | E | D | N | R |
| O | A | B | I | D | E |
| L | N | L | N | I | E |
| E | G | U | B | G | N |
| T | E | E | O | O | W |
| Y | E | L | L | O | W |

Now unscramble the letters you did NOT circle to answer this question:

**Where can you find all these colors in nature?**

**In a _ _ _ _ _ _ _ .**

# Language Arts

# Tell Me About It!

Read each group of words.
Underline the **statements**.

I like to go to the ice-cream store.

The pictures on the window.

My mother, my sister, and I.

We eat our favorite flavors.

The chocolate ice cream.

I sit on the bench.

## Brain Box

A **sentence** is a group
of words that express a
complete thought.

All sentences begin with a
capital letter.

A **statement** is a sentence
that explains or tells what
someone or something
does.

End a statement with a
period.

My mom likes vanilla.

The books resting by our feet.

I have red shoes.

the swimming class begins at noon

<u>The swimming class begins at noon.</u>

i can dive off the high board.

_____

Sara does a backflip

_____

the little kids wear water wings

_____

our lifeguard's name is Rena

_____

# Say What?

Rewrite each sentence.

If the sentence asks a **question,** add a question mark.

If the sentence is a **statement,** add a period.

is it raining hard

<u>Is it raining hard?</u>

sam likes his green boots

_____

can we jump in the puddles

_____

will you play with me after school

_____

i hope it stops raining

_____

what did the weather forecast say

_____

do you see a rainbow

_____

# Brain Box

A **question** is a sentence that asks something. End a question with a question mark.

Remember to begin all sentences with a capital letter.

# The Race Begins!

Rewrite each sentence as an **exclamation.**

look how fast I can run

<u>Look how fast I can run!</u>

tie your shoelaces

_____

we love racing

_____

on your mark, get set, go

_____

## Brain Box

hurry to the finish line

_____

An **exclamation** is a sentence that shows strong feelings, such as surprise, excitement, or fear. End an exclamation with an exclamation point.

Oh, no! Jamal is still reading when he should be going to sleep.

Write two **commands** that his father might say to him.

A **command** is a sentence that tells someone to do something. End a command with either a period or an exclamation point.

_____

_____

# A Picture Tells a Story

Write each sentence correctly.
Then circle the type of sentence it is.

Language
Arts

Types of
sentences

is the skateboard in the closet

Is the skateboard in the closet?

statement   (question)   exclamation   command

wear a hat and a sweater

_____

statement   question   exclamation   command

i think we should go to the park

_____

statement   question   exclamation   command

watch out for the ghost

_____

statement   question   exclamation   command

# Sentence Scramble

First, unscramble the words to write a **statement**.
Then use the same words to write a **question**.
Remember to **capitalize** and **punctuate**.

come  party
they  will
to  the

They will come to the party.
Will they come to the party?

Language
Arts

Word order

sleep  can
on  dog
bed  my  the

_____
_____

he  get
mail  should
the

_____
_____

Jane Smith
42 Maple Street
Townville, Kansas 55555

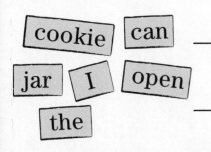

cookie  can
jar  I  open
the

_____
_____

cookies

# People in Town

Underline the **common nouns** in each sentence.

The boys ride bikes to the diner.

The girl looks through the window of the bookstore.

The man mows the grass in the park.

A woman feeds a duck near the pond.

My uncle pushes the swing on the playground.

My father buys broccoli at the market.

My mother drives her car to the office.

## Brain Box

A **common noun** is a word that names a person, place, or thing.

The children read books at school.

My aunt checks out a DVD at the library.

My grandmother eats cake at the bakery.

Now sort all the **common nouns**
you underlined on the cards.

people

boys
_____

places

diner
_____

things

bikes
_____

# And Away We Go!

Underline the **proper nouns** in each sentence.

**Language Arts**

Proper nouns

Dina walked across the Golden Gate Bridge in San Francisco.

In New York, Ramon went to the top of the Empire State Building.

Mrs. Li taught us that the Nile River is in Africa.

William went to Paris to see the painting of the Mona Lisa.

# Brain Box

A **proper noun** is a word that names a specific person, place, or thing.

**Proper nouns** are always capitalized.

Now fill in the box with the **proper nouns** you just underlined.

| People | Places | Things |
|--------|--------|--------|
| _____ | _____ | _____ |
| _____ | _____ | _____ |
| _____ | _____ | _____ |
| _____ | _____ | _____ |

Write a postcard to a friend about somewhere you have visited.

Circle all the **proper nouns.**

Dear _____,

_____

_____

_____

name

address

Sincerely,

_____

# Things I Like!

Fill in the notes with your favorite days.
Remember to capitalize each **proper noun.**

**Language Arts**

More proper nouns

My favorite holiday is:

_____

My favorite day of the week is:

_____

My birthday is:

_____

My favorite book is:

_____

My favorite movie is:

_____

My favorite TV show is:

_____

# Brain Box

The names of holidays, months, and days of the week are all **proper nouns.**

The titles of books, movies, TV shows, magazines, and newspapers are also proper nouns.

Remember to capitalize proper nouns.

# Fun at the Playground!

The words on the balls are all **pronouns.**

Rewrite each sentence using the pronoun that can take the place of the underlined word(s) in each sentence.

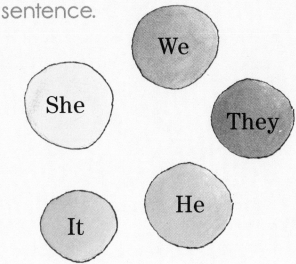

<u>Max and Lila</u> are on the seesaw.

**They are on the seesaw.**

<u>Juan</u> swings through the air.

_____

<u>Amy</u> zooms down the slide.

_____

<u>All of us</u> are having a good time.

_____

<u>The playground</u> is busy.

_____

## Brain Box

A **pronoun** is a word that can take the place of a noun.

# Dog Day

Underline the **subject** of each sentence.
Circle the **noun.**

The <u>park</u> is a busy place.

Ollie walks his dogs there every afternoon.

The biggest dog is named Hamlet.

Ollie's favorite is a poodle named Fifi.

The pets run and play together.

Some dogs bark at the squirrels.

The squirrels stay in the trees.

**Language Arts**

Subjects

## Brain Box

The **subject** tells who or what a sentence is about.

The **subject** always has a **noun** or a **pronoun** in it.

# Batter Up!

Use the words on the baseballs to complete the sentences.

 swings

The batter _____picks_____ up the bat.

 holds

She _____ up to home plate.

 hits

The catcher _____ up her mitt.

 steps

The pitcher _____ the ball.

 picks

The batter _____ .

throws

She _____ the ball.

Language Arts

Verbs

## Brain Box

A **verb** is an action word. It tells what someone or something does.

Write a sentence describing your favorite sport. Underline the **verb** in your sentence.

_____

_____

_____

# Now and Then

Underline the **verb** in each sentence.

Minx <u>jumps</u> up on the dresser.

Minx moves the book with her paw.

The book falls on the floor.

Jinx picks up the book.

He takes it into the living room.

Jinx licks the cover.

What will Jinx or Minx do next?
Write a sentence with a **present-tense verb.**
Underline the **verb** in your sentence.

_____

_____

_____

**Language Arts**

Present- and past-tense verbs

# Brain Box

A **present-tense verb** tells
what is happening now.

Minx and Jinx got into trouble yesterday, too!
Change the underlined **verb** to tell about the **past.**

Jinx <u>licks</u> his paw.

Yesterday, Jinx __licked__ his paw.

Jinx <u>chews</u> Marc's book.

Yesterday, Jinx _____ Marc's book.

Minx <u>claws</u> the cover.

Minx _____ the cover.

Marc <u>walks</u> into the room.

Marc _____ into the room.

He <u>picks</u> up the book.

He _____ up the book.

Marc <u>scolds</u> Jinx and Minx.

Marc _____ Jinx and Minx.

Marc <u>needs</u> a new book.

Marc _____ a new book.

Brain Quest Second Grade Workbook

**Language Arts**

Present- and past-tense verbs

## Brain Box

A **past-tense verb** tells what happened in the past.

You can add **ed** to many verbs to tell about actions that happened in the past.

# Time to Paint

Fill in the blanks with the correct form of the verb **to have.**

I **have** paints.   I ___had___ paints.

He **has** brushes.   He _____ brushes.

We _____ fun.   We **had** fun.

They **have** canvases.   They _____ canvases.

**Language Arts**

Irregular verbs: to have

Now use the correct form of the verb **to have** to answer these questions.

What color eyes do you have?

I _____ .

# Brain Box

The verb **to have** is irregular. This means it doesn't follow the same rules as most regular verbs.

**to have**

| present tense | | past tense |
|---|---|---|
| I **have** | = | I **had** |
| You **have** | = | You **had** |
| He / She / It **has** | = | He / She / It **had** |
| We / They **have** | = | We / They **had** |

What favorite toy did you

have as a baby?

I _____

_____ .

# Time for a Picnic!

Fill in the correct form of the verb **to be** to complete each sentence.
Color in PRESENT if the verb tells about the **present.**
Color in PAST if the verb tells about the **past.**

The picnic ___**was**___ last Sunday.

| present | past |
| --- | --- |

Today it _____ raining.

| present | past |
| --- | --- |

Luckily, the weather _____ dry last week.

| present | past |
| --- | --- |

We _____ in the park until it got dark.

| present | past |
| --- | --- |

I _____ tired when I got home from the picnic.

| present | past |
| --- | --- |

I _____ glad to be inside now.

| present | past |
| --- | --- |

## Brain Box

The verb **to be** is irregular. This means it doesn't follow the same rules as most regular verbs.

**to be**

| present tense | | past tense |
| --- | --- | --- |
| I **am** | = | I **was** |
| You **are** | = | You **were** |
| He / She / It **is** | = | He / She / It **was** |
| We / They **are** | = | We / They **were** |

# To Have and To Be

Use a form of **to be** or **to have** to answer each question.

Language
Arts

Irregular
verbs: to be,
to have

What is the weather like today?

_____

What was the weather like yesterday?

_____

Do you have an umbrella today?

_____

Draw a picture of you and a friend from school in the picture frame. Then answer the questions below.

I ___am___ _____8_____ years old.

My best friend _____ _____ years old.

This year, we _____ in the _____ grade.

Last year, we _____ in the _____ grade.

# Who Did What?

Use the drawings to help you match the **subjects** to the **predicates.**

Draw a line from the words in the SUBJECT column to the matching words in the PREDICATE column.

## Subject

The family

Lia

Ken

Their parents

## Predicate

painted the sign.

squeezed each one.

sold the lemonade.

cut the lemons in half.

Write sentences using the subjects and predicates you matched. Circle the noun(s) in the **subject.** Underline the verb in the **predicate.**

The (family) sold the lemonade.

_____

_____

_____

## Brain Box

The naming part of a sentence is called the **subject.** It tells who or what the sentence is about.

The telling part of a sentence is called the **predicate.** It tells what the subject does.

# Day at the Carnival

Look at each picture and read the caption.
Circle the **noun**.
Underline the **adjective**.

two prizes

white horse

red apples

tall clown

tiny lamb

## Brain Box

A **noun** names a person, place, or thing.

An **adjective** tells about or describes a noun.

Color, size, and number words are adjectives.

three flags

Write the **adjectives** under the correct headings on the chart.

Then, add two more adjectives to each list.

## ADJECTIVES

| Color Words | Number Words | Size Words |
|---|---|---|
| white | two | tiny |
| | | |
| | | |
| | | |

Write three sentences using all the new adjectives you added.

_____

_____

_____

_____

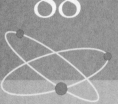

# Five Senses

Circle the **noun** in each caption.
Underline the **adjective.**

salty popcorn

loud noise

stinky cheese

wet elephant

colorful balloons

delicious hot dog

Write **look, feel, taste, smell,** or **sound** by the correct body parts below.

smell

# Brain Box

**Adjectives** can tell how nouns look, feel, taste, smell, or sound.

# Where? When? How?

The **verb** in each sentence has been underlined. Circle the **adverb.**

(Yesterday) we <u>found</u> the treasure map.

It <u>was hidden</u> upstairs.

We <u>screamed</u> loudly when we found it.

Now we <u>will hunt</u> for treasure.

The treasure <u>is buried</u> under the tree.

<u>Can</u> we <u>find</u> it quickly?

Write each **adverb** you circled on the correct card below.

Language Arts

Adverbs

## Brain Box

**Adverbs** tell where, when, or how something happens.

An **adverb** can tell more about a **verb.**

Example: Tomorrow, we will eat ice cream.

**Tomorrow** is the adverb because it tells when we will eat ice cream.

Where?

_____

_____

When?

<u>yesterday</u>

_____

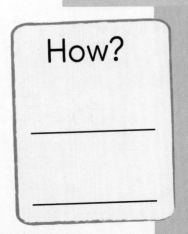

How?

_____

_____

# Bear Bakes

Underline the **verb** in each sentence.
Circle the **adverb.**

Language
Arts

Adverbs

Bear <u>went</u> (inside) to bake apples.

He washed the apples carefully.

Afterward, he put them in the oven.

Later, he saw they were done.

He took the tray from the oven slowly.

He will sell the apples outside at the market.

Write each **adverb** you circled on the correct card below.

**Where?**

inside

**When?**

**How?**

# Reading

# A Poem

Read the poem.

## Bed in Summer

### Robert Louis Stevenson

In winter I get up at night
And dress by yellow candlelight.
In summer, quite the other way,
I have to go to bed by day.

I have to go to bed and see
The birds still hopping on the tree,
Or hear the grown-up people's feet
Still going past me in the street.

And does it not seem hard to you,
When all the sky is clear and blue,
And I should like so much to play,
To have to go to bed by day?

"Bed in Summer" is a poem that rhymes.
Fill in the chart with **rhyming words** that end the lines
of the poem. Then add your own rhyming word.

night

way

see

feet

you

Now answer the questions.

**How does the child in the poem feel?**

_____

_____

**How do you feel in the summertime?**

_____

_____

# A Fable

Read the story.
Answer the questions for each part of the story.

# The Wind and the Sun

## An Aesop Fable

One bright, sunny day, Wind blew in. The trees bowed down. The windows in a farmhouse shook.

Wind boasted, "I am Wind and I am strong! I am stronger than trees. I am stronger than windows. I am stronger than Sun!"

Sun came out from behind a cloud. Sun said, "Wind, you are strong. But I am stronger than you."

"No!" said Wind. "I am stronger than you!"

Sun said, "Let us have a contest to see who is stronger."

– 1 –

"Yes!" said Wind. "We will have a contest!"

Sun looked down and saw an old man strolling by. He wore a hat and an overcoat. "Do you see that old man?" Sun asked. "Whichever of us can make him take off his overcoat is the strongest. Wind, I will let you go first." Then Sun hid behind a cloud to watch.

Wind huffed. Wind puffed. Wind began to blow. The trees bowed down even lower. The windows in the farmhouse shook louder. Wind blew strong and cold.

The man said, "Brrr! What a cold, strong wind!" Then he buttoned up his overcoat.

Wind blew stronger. Wind blew colder.

– 2 –

(continued on next page)

# Who are the main characters in the story?

_____

_____

**Reading**

Reading skills

With each gust of cold air, the old man stayed huddled inside his overcoat.

Sun came out from behind the cloud. "Now it is my turn." Sun smiled. Bright rays of sunlight filled the air. The air grew warmer.

The old man said, "Ah! The sun feels nice and warm." Then he unbuttoned his overcoat.

Sun shone brighter and brighter. The old man felt warmer and warmer. He said, "The sun is very strong. I feel very warm. I do not need my overcoat." And the old man took off his overcoat.

Sun said, "I win."

"You win this time," Wind said. "Next time, *I* will pick the contest!"

THE END

– 3 –

What do Sun and Wind want to do?

_____

_____

What happened when Wind blew?

_____

_____

What happened when Sun shone?

_____

_____

Who won the contest?

_____

What would happen if Rain came along and entered the contest?

_____

_____

How does having a contest solve an argument?

_____

_____

# What's Cooking?

Read the recipes.

Make up a name for each recipe. Write it on the line.

Reading

Reading recipes

_____
**recipe name**

**INGREDIENTS:**
• banana
• blueberries
• grapes
• strawberries

**DIRECTIONS:**
1. Slice the banana into round pieces.
2. Wash the blueberries, grapes, and strawberries.
3. Slice the strawberries in half.
4. Mix the fruit in a bowl.

_____
**recipe name**

**INGREDIENTS:**
• banana
• slice of bread
• peanut butter

**DIRECTIONS:**
1. Slice the banana into round pieces.
2. Toast a slice of bread.
3. Spread peanut butter on the toast.
4. Put the banana slices on top of the peanut butter.

_____
**recipe name**

**INGREDIENTS:**
• banana
• $\frac{1}{2}$ cup vanilla yogurt
• $\frac{1}{4}$ cup granola

**DIRECTIONS:**
1. Cut the banana into small pieces.
2. Put the yogurt in a bowl.
3. Sprinkle the fruit and granola on top.

What dish can you make?
List the ingredients.
Write the steps in order.
Draw a picture of the dish.
Give your dish a name.

_____
**recipe name**

**INGREDIENTS:**

_____

_____

_____

_____

**DIRECTIONS:**

1. _____

2. _____

3. _____

4. _____

# Yum!

# A Myth

Read the story.
Answer the questions for each part of the story.

**Reading**

Reading skills

## How Day and Night Came to Be

**An Inuit Myth**

When the world was very young, there was only darkness. Ice covered the land. Two children, a boy and a girl, lived in a small cabin. They hunted for food. It was hard work. It was tiring work. There was no time to play.

One day, a stranger came to their door. He was part man, part raven. He asked the children to come out and play. The children were too tired to play. They offered the Raven Man food and drink.

"No, thank you," said the Raven Man.

— 1 —

**Why was there no time for the children to play?**

_____

_____

"But if you can solve this puzzle, I will reward you." He gave them a small bag and left.

In the bag were many small fish bones. By the pale light of a small lamp, the children arranged the bones into the shape of the fish. They solved the Raven Man's puzzle.

Their reward was a fishing spear. The sharp barbs on the spear made hunting easier. Then the Raven Man gave the children a second puzzle of bones. The children put the pieces together to make the flipper of a seal. Again, the Raven Man rewarded them.

The Raven Man's second gift was an oil lamp large enough for cooking and heating. With each gift, the Raven Man

– 2 –

(continued on next page)

made life a little easier for the children. Then the Raven Man took out a ball. He said, "Now let's play."

Outside in the freezing darkness, the children and the Raven Man played catch. Suddenly the ball caught on the Raven Man's sharp beak. The ball ripped open. Through the tear, the sun escaped and lit the sky. For the first time, the world felt the warmth of sunshine.

And that is how day was created out of night.

THE END

– 3 –

What was inside the ball the children were playing with?

_____

_____

What two gifts did the Raven Man give the children?

_____

_____

How do you think the children feel at the end of the story? Why?

_____

_____

How would this story ending be different if the visitor were a Rabbit Man instead of the Raven Man?

_____

_____

What happened first, next, and last?
Number the pictures to show the order.

# A Folktale

Read the play out loud, by yourself, or with friends. Then answer the questions at the end of the play.

Reading

Reading a play

## Buying the Shade

### A Folktale

STORYTELLER: Once there lived a mean, rich old man. One afternoon, the mean old man took a nap under a tree near his house. When he woke up, he saw a young man also enjoying the shade.

OLD MAN: Go away, young man! This is my shade!

YOUNG MAN: Sir? Why is this your shade? I thought this tree belonged to the village.

OLD MAN: Ha! My great-great-grandfather planted this tree! This tree and its shade belong only to me!

STORYTELLER: The young man thought, "I shall teach the old man a lesson."

YOUNG MAN: Then, sir, I wish to buy the shade from your tree.

STORYTELLER: The old man thought, "I shall take the young man's gold!"

OLD MAN: You may buy my shade for five pieces of gold!

YOUNG MAN: Done!

STORYTELLER: Now the old man was quite pleased with himself. He was five pieces of gold richer. He put the gold in his pocket and went back to his big house.

Later that afternoon, the sun began to set. The shadow of the tree grew and grew, until it covered the old man's house. The young man walked into the old man's house.

OLD MAN: What are you doing in my house? Get out of here!

YOUNG MAN: The shade of the tree covers this house. The shade belongs to me. Now the house belongs to me, too.

STORYTELLER: In anger, the old man left the village forever. The clever young man moved into the big house.

YOUNG MAN (to the whole village): People, please come and enjoy the shade of the tree!

STORYTELLER: And they did.

**Reading**

Reading
a play

Plot the play you just read.
Tell what happens in the **beginning, middle,** and **end** of the play.

**Reading**

Reading
a play

Beginning | Why won't the old man let the young man rest under the tree?

_____

_____

_____

Middle | What does the young man do next?

_____

_____

_____

End | How does the story end?

_____

_____

_____

Can you think of a different ending for the story? Write it here.

_____

_____

_____

Read the story.

## Monday Morning

One Monday morning, Lena turned off the radio and put an umbrella in her backpack. The backpack was so stuffed, the umbrella stuck out.

On her way to school, Lena saw her friends Grace and Justin. "Hey, Lena," called Grace. "Wait up."

Grace and Justin caught up with Lena.

"What's that sticking out of your backpack?" asked Grace.

"My umbrella," said Lena. "What's that sticking out of your backpack?"

"My soccer shin guards," Grace said. "We have practice today."

"I don't think so," said Lena.

"We always have soccer practice on Mondays," said Justin.

– 1 –

(continued on next page)

## Brain Box

A **cause** tells why something happens.

An **effect** is what happens.

"Not when it rains," Lena said.

The three children looked up at the sun in the bright blue sky.

"It won't rain today," said Grace.

"I listened to the radio this morning," Lena said.

"And what did the weather report say?" Justin asked. "Did it say there will be no soccer practice this afternoon?"

Lena laughed. "Well, almost! The forecast is for thunderstorms this afternoon."

THE END

Draw a line to match each **cause** and **effect**.

## Causes

## Effects

Lena learned it was going to rain.

They put their shin guards in their backpacks.

Grace and Justin play soccer on Monday.

They talk and joke together.

Lena, Grace, and Justin are friends.

She took an umbrella to school.

Write three other titles for this story.
Circle the one you like best.

_____

_____

_____

# Telling Tall Tales

Read the stories.

**Paul Bunyan** was born in Maine, but he grew so big and tall that he outgrew the state and headed west. During a terrible blizzard in the Midwest, Paul went out for a walk. In a snowdrift, he heard a sound. Paul reached into the snow and pulled out a blue ox. Paul named the ox Babe.

Paul was a lumberjack. With Babe the Blue Ox at his side, Paul and other lumberjacks cleared the trees in the Midwest so farmers could use the land. Paul dug a few ponds for drinking water for his crew. Today we call those ponds the Great Lakes!

**Pecos Bill** was born in Texas. When he was just a little baby, his parents traveled west. Baby Bill fell out of the family wagon and got lost. Lucky for Bill, a family of coyotes found him. The coyotes raised him as one of their own.

Bill was the first cowboy. On a bet, he rode a cyclone without a saddle. It never did throw him. That poor cyclone rained itself out. The rain fell so hard and so heavy that it carved out the Grand Canyon!

# Who is who?

Write the name of the character in the picture on the line.

_____

_____

_____

_____

# A Folktale

Read the story. Then answer the questions.

## Anansi and the Talking Melon

### A Folktale from Africa

Long, long ago in Africa, there lived a spider named Anansi. He was clever but also very lazy. Anansi made his home in a thorn tree that overlooked Elephant's melon patch. Every day, Elephant weeded and watered the melons. Every day, the melons grew bigger and riper. Every day, Anansi's appetite for melons grew bigger, too.

 One hot summer afternoon, Elephant weeded and watered his melon patch. Then he left the garden. Anansi really wanted one of Elephant's melons!

What do you think Anansi will do next?

I predict that Anansi will _____

_____

_____

Reading

Reading skills

Anansi took a thorn from his thorn tree and lowered himself into Elephant's garden. Clever Anansi picked the best melon. He used the thorn to make a hole in it. Then the hungry spider crawled inside.

Anansi ate. He ate and ate and ate, until he could eat no more. Finally, Anansi tried to crawl out of the hole. But he was stuck! He had eaten too much, and now the hole was too small. How would Anansi get out?

**What is Anansi's problem?**

_____

_____

**What caused Anansi's problem?**

_____

_____

The clever spider thought up a clever plan. As Elephant walked by the melon, Anansi said loudly and clearly, "I am the king!"

"Who said that?" asked Elephant.

"I did," said Anansi from inside the melon. "I am the king!"

Reading

Reading skills

Surprised, Elephant said, "You're a melon, not a king! But a talking melon is rare. I will take you to the king."

Elephant presented the melon to the king. The king said, "Why have you brought me a melon, Elephant? I have melons of my own."

"Not like this one, Your Majesty," said Elephant.

Then the melon said, "I am the king!"

"Who said that?" demanded the king angrily.

How does the king feel? Why does he feel that way?

_____

_____

"I did," said the melon. "I am the king!"

"You are not the king! You are a melon!" roared the king. Then the king took the melon and threw it.

The melon sailed through the air all the way back to Elephant's garden. The melon landed SPLAT! and cracked wide open. Anansi jumped out and scurried up a coconut tree.

Elephant returned home. He said to his melons, "You are melons. Just melons! Not kings!"

From behind a coconut, Anansi said, "Melon kings! How silly!"

Elephant looked up into his coconut tree and cried, "Oh, no! Talking coconuts!"

THE END

How did Anansi solve his problem?

_____

_____

# Imagine That!

Write your own poem, fable, myth, short story, folktale, or play on the page below.

Don't forget to write the title on the first line.

_____

_____

_____

_____

_____

_____

_____

_____

_____

# Writing

# Alien Interview

Write a **question** for each human to ask the alien about life on another planet.

Who _____

_____ ?

What _____

_____ ?

Where _____

_____ ?

Why _____

_____ ?

When _____

_____ ?

How _____

_____ ?

Write an **answer** from the alien for each question.

Writing

# What a Day!

Imagine you were one of the kids who met the alien from another planet.

Write about what you and your new alien friend did.

Dear Diary,

_____

_____

_____

_____

_____

_____ ,

_____
**your name**

# What Is a Wocnix?

**Wocnix** is a made-up word.

What do you think it is? A flower? An animal?

You decide. Draw a picture of a wocnix in the box.

Wocnix

Write sentences to describe the wocnix.

What does it look like? _____

_____

What does it sound like? _____

_____

What does it feel like? _____

_____

How does it taste? _____

How does it smell? _____

# Fill Me In!

Read the story and fill in the missing words.
Give your story a title.

Title: _____

Today is _____ , the first day of
             day of the week

_____ vacation. I put on my favorite
        season

_____ . _____ and I made
        clothing              family member

_____ for _____ .
        food                    meal

It tasted _____ ! Then we went to
            how something tastes

_____ . The first thing we did
      fun place

was _____ . After that, we
             activity #1

_____ . By the time we got
        activity #2

home, it was _____ .
                    time of day

What a _____ day!
              adjective

Draw a picture to go with your story.

**Writing**

Word
categories

# Step by Step

Read the recipe.

## SUPER SUNDAE

**Ingredients:**

- banana
- vanilla ice cream
- chocolate ice cream
- strawberry ice cream
- chocolate sauce
- whipped cream

**Directions:**

1. Slice the banana lengthwise.

2. Put the banana in the bowl.

3. Add 1 scoop of vanilla, 1 scoop of chocolate, and 1 scoop of strawberry.

4. Cover with chocolate sauce.

5. Add whipped cream.

How do you make your favorite food?
Write the recipe here.

**Recipe Name**

**Ingredients:**

- _____    - _____

- _____    - _____

- _____    - _____

**Directions:**

1. _____

2. _____

3. _____

4. _____

5. _____

# Be Critical

Follow the steps below to write
your own book review.

Book title: _____

Author: _____

Reviewed by: _____

**What is the book about?**

_____

_____

**What did you like about the book?**
**Give a reason for your opinion.**

_____

_____

**What didn't you like?**
**Give a reason for your opinion.**

_____

_____

**What happened in your favorite part of the book?**

_____

_____

Writing

Reviews

Movie title: _____

Starring: _____

Reviewed by: _____

What is the movie about?

_____

_____

What did you like about the movie?
Give a reason for your opinion.

_____

_____

What didn't you like?
Give a reason for your opinion.

_____

_____

What happened in your favorite part of the movie?

_____

_____

## Brain Box

A **review** tells what the reader or viewer thinks about a book or movie.

# And Then . . .

Read the beginning of the story.
Write about what happens next.
Then draw a picture.

I woke up early because my back itched. I got
out of bed and looked in the mirror. I couldn't
believe my eyes! I had wings!

_____

_____

_____

_____

**Writing**

Story starters

The balloon seller handed me a brown balloon. He winked and said, "Be careful. This one is magic!"

_____

_____

_____

_____

My friends and I played hide-and-seek in the park.
I hid behind a big oak tree. I saw a small sign on
the trunk. It said: KNOCK TWO TIMES. So I did.

_____

_____

_____

_____

# Cursive

# A Is for Alexis

Trace the letters. Then write them.

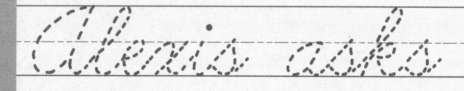

a a a

a a a

a a a

**Cursive**

A, a

Trace the sentence.

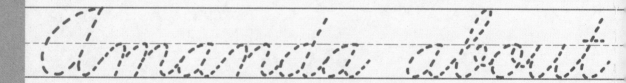

*Alexis asks*

*Amanda about*

*Alaska.*

# B Is for Ben

Trace the letters. Then write them.

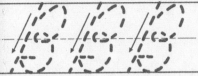

Trace the sentence.

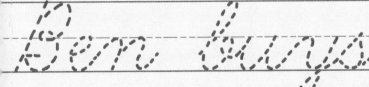

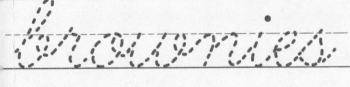

Cursive

B b

# C Is for Carmen

Trace the letters. Then write them.

Cursive

C c

Trace the sentence.

*Carmen can canoe. Can you?*

Trace the letters. Then write them.

*D D D*

*d d d*

*d d d*

Trace the sentence.

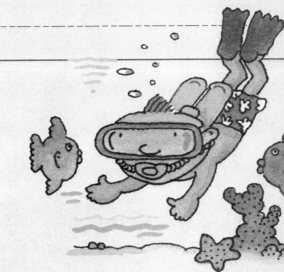

Cursive

D d

*David dives*

*down into the*

*deep sea.*

# E Is for Eric

Trace the letters. Then write them.

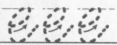

E e

Trace the sentence.

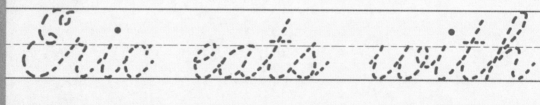

Eric eats with Edna the elephant.

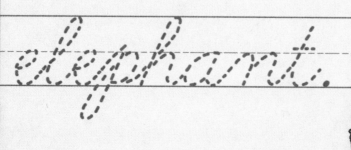

# F Is for Francesca

Trace the letters. Then write them.

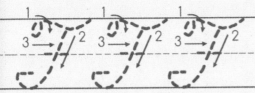

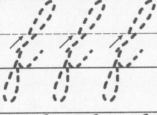

**Cursive**

F, f

Trace the sentence.

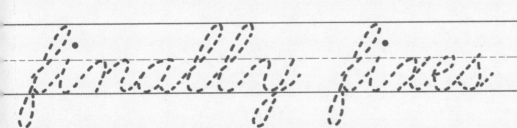

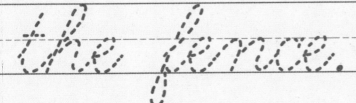

# G Is for Garret

Trace the letters. Then write them.

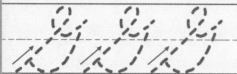

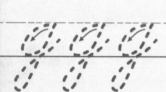

Trace the sentence.

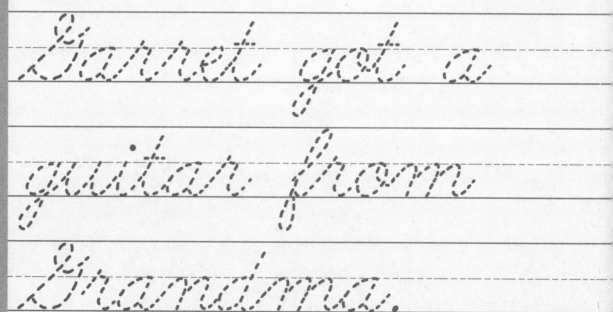

*Garret got a guitar from Grandma.*

# H Is for Hannah

Trace the letters. Then write them.

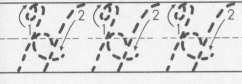

Trace the sentence.

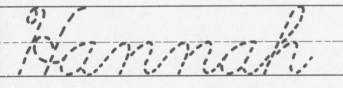

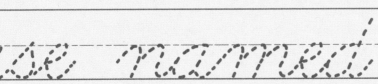

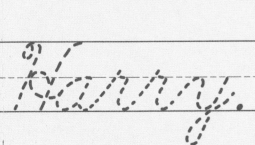

**Cursive**

H, h

# I Is for Ina

Trace the letters. Then write them.

*I I I*

*i i i*

*i i i*

**Cursive**

I i

Trace the sentence.

*Ina ice-skates*

*around an*

*igloo.*

# J Is for Juan

Trace the letters. Then write them.

*J J J*

*j j j*

*j j j*

**Cursive**

Trace the sentence.

*Juan just put the jellyfish in the jar.*

Brain Quest Second Grade Workbook

# K Is for Kayla

Trace the letters. Then write them.

**Cursive**

K k

Trace the sentence.

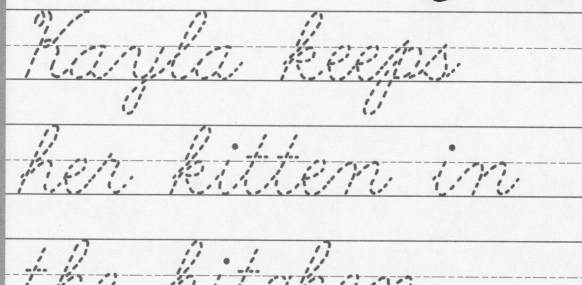

*Kayla keeps
her kitten in
the kitchen.*

# L Is for Lauren

Trace the letters. Then write them.

*L L L*

*l l l*

*l l l*

**Cursive**

L l

Trace the sentence.

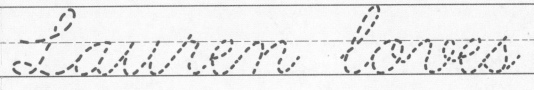

*Lauren loves*

*lemons and*

*limes.*

# M Is for Manuel

Trace the letters. Then write them.

Trace the sentence.

*Manuel makes a monster mask.*

# N Is for Nicole

Trace the letters. Then write them.

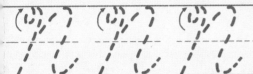

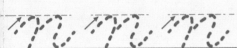

Trace the sentence.

Cursive

N n

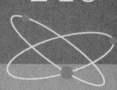

# O Is for Omar

Trace the letters. Then write them.

Trace the sentence.

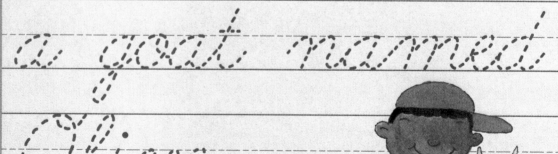

# P Is for Pia

Trace the letters. Then write them.

*P P P P*

*p p p*

*p p p*

Trace the sentence.

*Pia paints*

*a pig named*

*Petunia.*

# Q Is for Quinn

Trace the letters. Then write them.

2 2 2

q q q

q q q

Trace the sentence.

Quinn eats a quarter of the quiche.

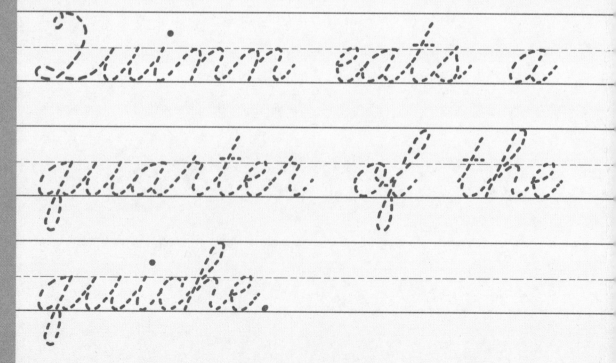

# R Is for Rajeev

Trace the letters. Then write them.

*R R R*

*r r r*

*r r r*

Trace the sentence.

*Rajeev reads about rowdy rabbits.*

**Cursive**

R,r

# S Is for Shantel

Trace the letters. Then write them.

Trace the sentence.

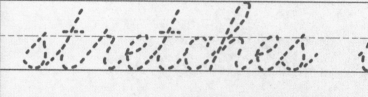

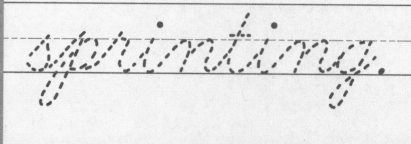

# T Is for Trung

Trace the letters. Then write them.

$\mathscr{T}$ $\mathscr{T}$ $\mathscr{T}$

$t$ $t$ $t$

$t$ $t$ $t$

Trace the sentence.

Trung sets up his tent under the tree.

Cursive

Tt

151

# U Is for Uma

Trace the letters. Then write them.

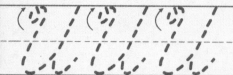

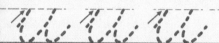

**Cursive**

U u

Trace the sentence.

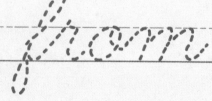

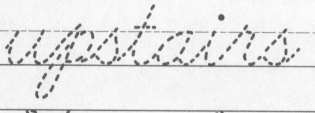

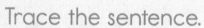

# V Is for Victor

Trace the letters. Then write them.

*VVV*

*VVV*

*VVV*

Trace the sentence.

*Victor visits*

*Velma and*

*Vance.*

# W Is for William

Trace the letters. Then write them.

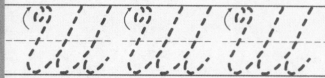

Trace the sentence.

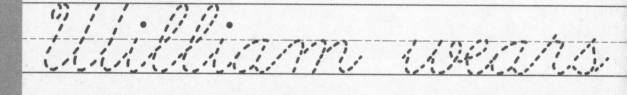

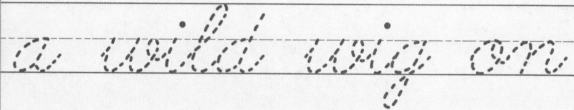

# X Is for Xena

Trace the letters. Then write them.

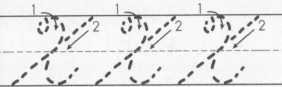

Trace the sentence.

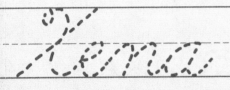

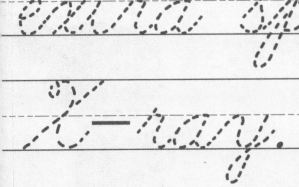

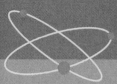

# Y Is for Yolanda

Trace the letters. Then write them.

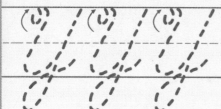

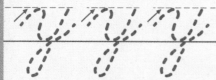

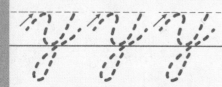

**Cursive**

Y y

Trace the sentence.

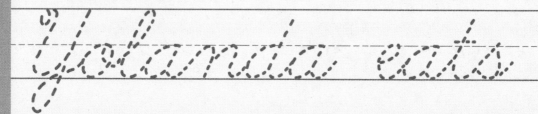

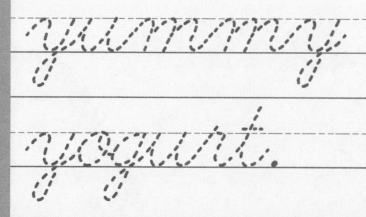

# Z Is for Zack

Trace the letters. Then write them.

Trace the sentence.

**Cursive**

Z z

*Zack feeds a zebra at the zoo.*

# More Letters

Write your first name in cursive on the lines.
Draw a star next to the one you like best.

Write your last name in cursive on the lines.
Draw a star next to the one you like best.

# More About Me

Use your best handwriting to write the names of:

Your parent(s):

Sibling(s):

Pet(s):

# My Favorite Things

Use your best handwriting to name your favorite:

Book:

Movie:

TV show:

Food:

Sport:

Color:

# Math Skills

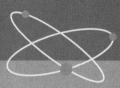

# Bundles of Bugs

Look at the **numerals** and words on each jar.
Write the number they equal on the line.

 1 ten **+**  7 ones **=** <u>17</u>

 3 tens **+**  8 ones **=** _____

 7 tens **+**  0 ones **=** _____

**Math Skills**

Place value to tens

 9 tens **+**  3 ones **=** _____

# Brain Box

You can use **place value** to figure out how much numerals are worth. Look at **36:**

| tens | ones |
|------|------|
| 3 | 6 |

The **3** tells us there are **3** tens.
The **6** tells us there are **6** ones.

# Hop to It!

Circle the correct **numeral.**

Circle the ones.      12③

Circle the tens.      45

Circle the hundreds.      836

Circle the tens.      517

Circle the hundreds.      382

Circle the ones.      697

Write the place value for each numeral on the chart.

| | hundreds | tens | ones |
|---|---|---|---|
| 624 | 6 | 2 | 4 |
| 391 | ___ | ___ | ___ |
| 105 | ___ | ___ | ___ |
| 879 | ___ | ___ | ___ |
| 243 | ___ | ___ | ___ |

**Math Skills**

Place value to hundreds

## Brain Box

If you see three numerals, you know that the number is made up of hundreds, tens, and ones. Look at **834**:

hundreds | tens | ones

8 | 3 | 4

The **8** tells us there are **8** hundreds. The **3** tells us there are **3** tens. The **4** tells us there are **4** ones.

# Lucky Thousands

Write the **place value** for each numeral on the chart.

| | thousands | hundreds | tens | ones |
|---|---|---|---|---|
| 1,843 | 1 | 8 | 4 | 3 |
| 2,692 | | | | |
| 7,034 | | | | |
| 4,880 | | | | |
| 9,718 | | | | |

Draw a line to match the words to the number.

8 thousands, 5 hundreds, 3 tens, 5 ones          9,101

9 thousands, 1 hundred, 0 tens, 1 one          6,464

6 thousands, 4 hundreds, 4 tens, 6 ones          6,446

6 thousands, 4 hundreds, 6 tens, 4 ones          8,535

**Math Skills**

Place value to thousands

# Brain Box

If you see four numerals, you know that the number is made up of thousands, hundreds, tens, and ones. Look at **4,627**:

| thousands | hundreds | tens | ones |
|---|---|---|---|
| 4 | 6 | 2 | 7 |

The **4** tells us there are **4** thousands. The **6** tells us there are **6** hundreds. The **2** tells us there are **2** tens. The **7** tells us there are **7** ones.

# Words to Numbers

Draw a line to match the number to the words.

 21

 1,586

 310

 301

 1,856

 12

1 ten and 2 ones

3 hundreds and 1 ten

1 thousand, 5 hundreds, 8 tens, and 6 ones

2 tens and 1 one

3 hundreds and 1 one

1 thousand, 8 hundreds, 5 tens, and 6 ones

**Math Skills**

Place value

Write out the number **452** using words:

_____

_____

# 166

# Words to Numbers

Write the numbers on the apples.

fifty-seven  _57_

thirty-two  ____

one hundred sixty-five  ____

seven hundred twelve  ____

five hundred eighty-three  ____

nine hundred six  ____

two thousand six hundred nineteen  ____

When do you use a comma when writing numbers?

_____

Where does the comma belong?

_____

**Math Skills**

Write the
numerals

# My Numbers

Write how many of each you have
in the chart below.

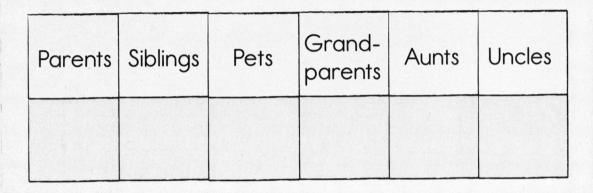

| Parents | Siblings | Pets | Grand-parents | Aunts | Uncles |
|---------|----------|------|---------------|-------|--------|
|         |          |      |               |       |        |

Which do you have the most of? _____

Least? _____

Are any the same number? _____

Complete the sentences with numbers.
Then write the numbers in words.

I am _____ years old. _____

I am _____ inches tall. _____

I weigh _____ pounds. _____

**Math Skills**

Personal
numbers

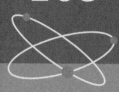

# You're Invited!

All the numbers are spelled out in fancy invitations. Finish this fancy invitation to your next birthday party. Spell out all the numbers.

_____
your name

will be _____ years old on
             age

_____ _____ ,
month                  day

_____
year

Where: _____
            street address

_____ , _____
city                  state

When: _____
           date

At: _____
      time

# Compare the Candles

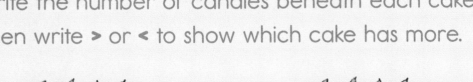

Write the number of candles beneath each cake.
Then write > or < to show which cake has more.

$$\underline{12} \quad < \quad \underline{13}$$

_____    _____    _____

_____    _____    _____

_____    _____    _____

_____    _____    _____

**Math Skills**

Greater than, less than

## Brain Box

< means **less than.**

> means **greater than.**

Example: **4 < 6**

The **less than** sign tells us that **4** is less than **6.**

Example: **10 > 5**

The **greater than** sign tells us that **10** is greater than **5.**

# Guess My Age

Write > or < to show who is older.

$<$

_____

**Math Skills**

Greater than,
less than

_____

_____

# Count by Twos!

Fill in the missing numbers on the pearl necklace.

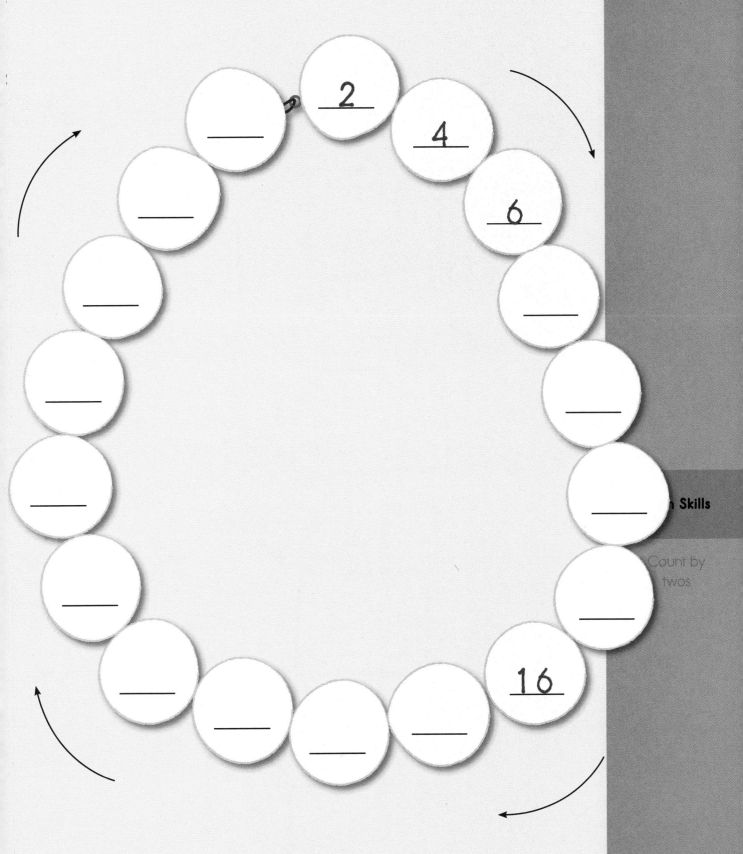

# 172

# Count by Threes!

Fill in the missing numbers on the blocks.

**Math Skills**

Count by
threes

3

___

___

___

15

___

___

___

# Count by Fours!

Start at **4.** Write the missing numbers on the cars.

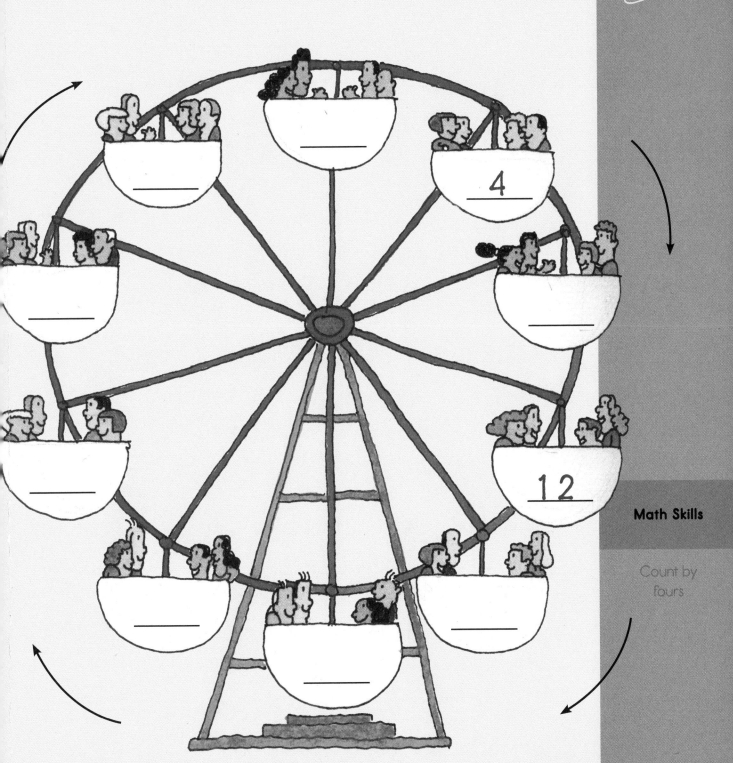

If there were 4 more cars on the Ferris wheel, what number would be on the last car?

# Count by Fives!

Write the missing numbers on the flags.

**Row 1:** 5  \_\_\_  \_\_\_  20  \_\_\_  \_\_\_  \_\_\_

**Row 2:** 40  \_\_\_  55  \_\_\_  \_\_\_  \_\_\_

**Row 3:** 75  \_\_\_  \_\_\_  \_\_\_  \_\_\_  100

If the third row had 6 more flags,

what number would be last?

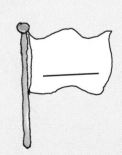

# Count by Tens!

Write the missing numbers on the shirts.

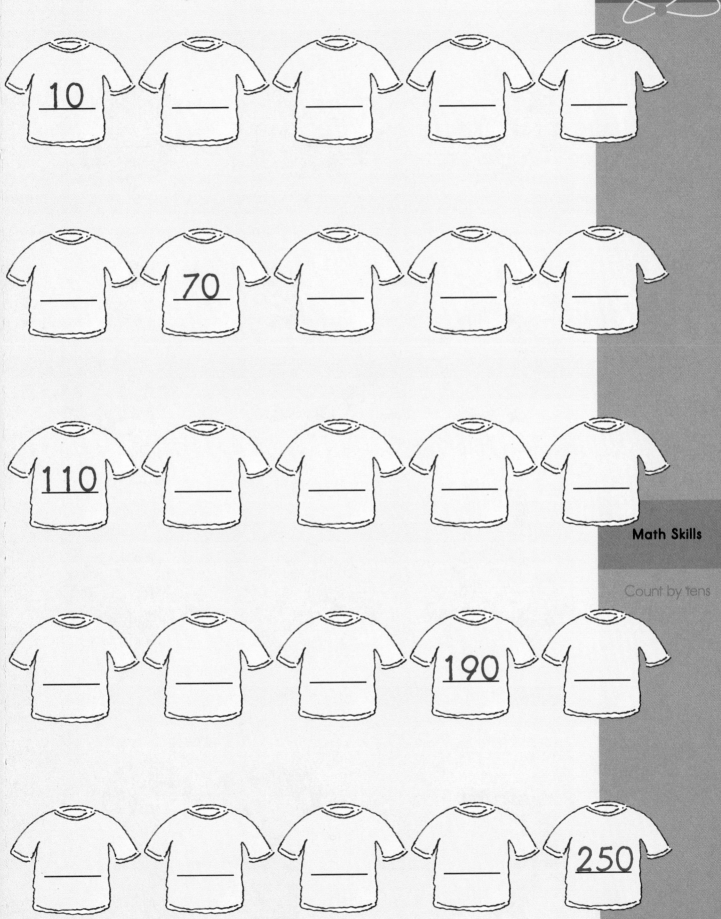

Row 1: 10, ___, ___, ___, ___

Row 2: ___, 70, ___, ___, ___

Row 3: 110, ___, ___, ___, ___

Row 4: ___, ___, ___, 190, ___

Row 5: ___, ___, ___, ___, 250

**Math Skills**

Count by tens

# Count by Hundreds!

Write the missing numbers on the suns.

 100    ____    ____

 ____    ____    600

 ____    800    ____

 ____

# Addition and Subtraction

# Pop That Balloon!

**Add** the numbers in each balloon.

If all the sums equal the number on the basket, color the balloon any color you like.

If the sums do not equal the number on the basket, pop the balloon by coloring it black.

$6 + 2 = \underline{\phantom{00}}$

$4 + 4 = \underline{\phantom{00}}$

$2 + 6 = \underline{\phantom{00}}$

$2 + 7 = \underline{\phantom{00}}$

$1 + 3 = \underline{\phantom{00}}$

$2 + 2 = \underline{\phantom{00}}$

$4 + 0 = \underline{\phantom{00}}$

$3 + 1 = \underline{\phantom{00}}$

$4 + 3 = \underline{\phantom{00}}$

$2 + 5 = \underline{\phantom{00}}$

$5 + 2 = \underline{\phantom{00}}$

$3 + 4 = \underline{\phantom{00}}$

8

4

7

**Addition and Subtraction**

Adding single-digit numbers

8 + 7 = _____

6 + 9 = _____

7 + 8 = _____

5 + 9 = _____

5 + 5 = _____

7 + 3 = _____

8 + 2 = _____

2 + 8 = _____

15

10

3 + 9 = _____

9 + 3 = _____

7 + 5 = _____

8 + 4 = _____

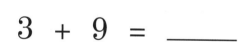

3 + 3 = _____

4 + 1 = _____

1 + 4 = _____

2 + 4 = _____

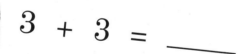

**Addition and Subtraction**

Adding
single-digit
numbers

12

6

Brain Quest Second Grade Workbook

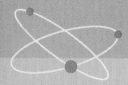

# Go Fish!

Finish the **fact families.** Write the missing numbers.

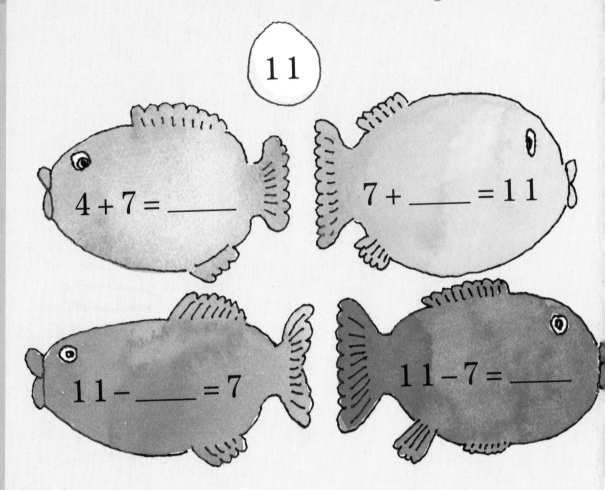

11

$4 + 7 = \underline{\hphantom{00}}$

$7 + \underline{\hphantom{00}} = 11$

$11 - \underline{\hphantom{00}} = 7$

$11 - 7 = \underline{\hphantom{00}}$

**Addition and Subtraction**

Fact families

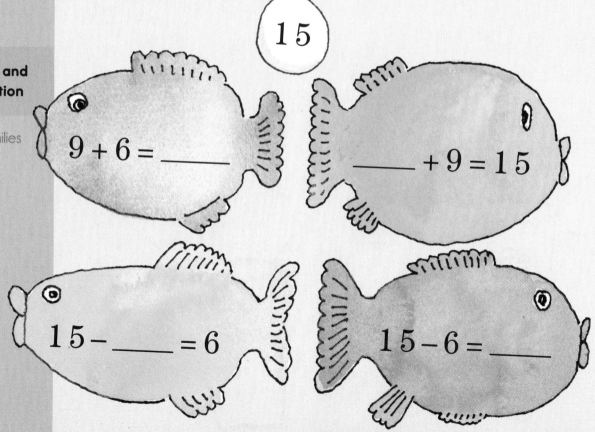

15

$9 + 6 = \underline{\hphantom{00}}$

$\underline{\hphantom{00}} + 9 = 15$

$15 - \underline{\hphantom{00}} = 6$

$15 - 6 = \underline{\hphantom{00}}$

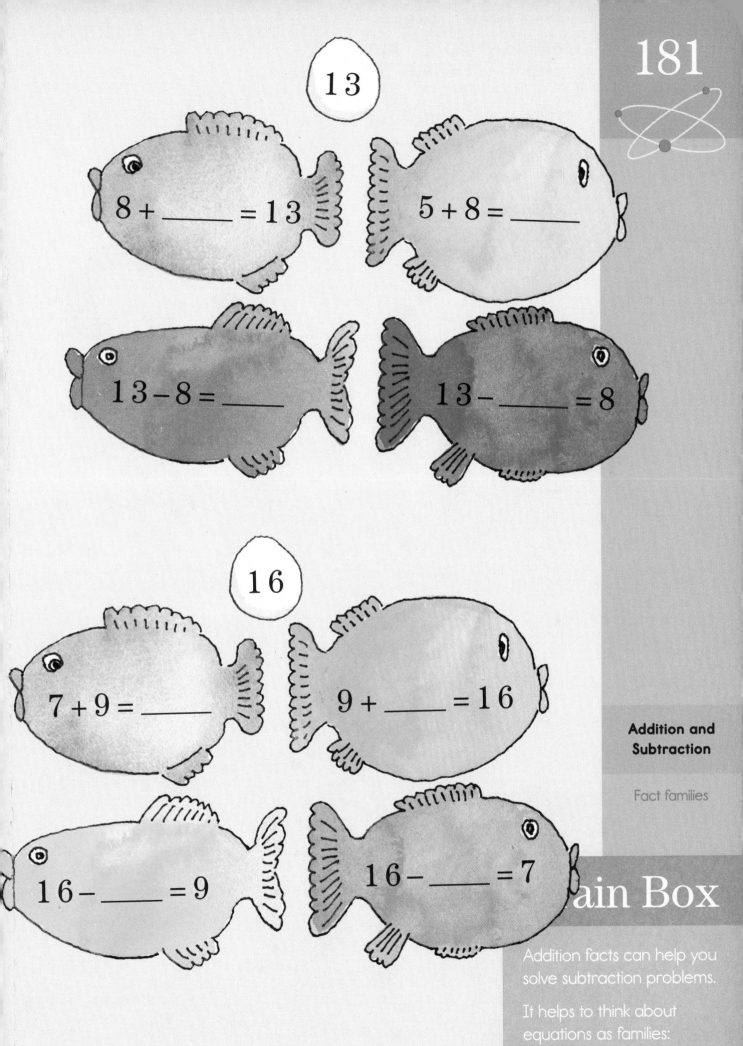

$13$

$8 + \underline{\hspace{1cm}} = 13$

$5 + 8 = \underline{\hspace{1cm}}$

$13 - 8 = \underline{\hspace{1cm}}$

$13 - \underline{\hspace{1cm}} = 8$

$16$

$7 + 9 = \underline{\hspace{1cm}}$

$9 + \underline{\hspace{1cm}} = 16$

$16 - \underline{\hspace{1cm}} = 9$

$16 - \underline{\hspace{1cm}} = 7$

**Addition and Subtraction**

Fact families

**ain Box**

Addition facts can help you solve subtraction problems.

It helps to think about equations as families:

$6 + 2 = 8 \qquad 8 - 2 = 6$
$2 + 6 = 8 \qquad 8 - 6 = 2$

# Tic Tac Total

**Add** each set of numbers. To win tic-tac-toe, draw a line through the three answers that are the same.

| | | |
|---|---|---|
| 11<br>+ 6 | 23<br>+ 15 | 14<br>+ 4 |
| 17<br>+ 22 | 14<br>+ 3 | 21<br>+ 16 |
| 20<br>+ 39 | 23<br>+ 5 | 10<br>+ 7 |

| | | |
|---|---|---|
| 27<br>+ 22 | 14<br>+ 5 | 21<br>+ 4 |
| 10<br>+ 8 | 20<br>+ 5 | 13<br>+ 6 |
| 22<br>+ 3 | 10<br>+ 7 | 28<br>+ 31 |

**Addition and Subtraction**

# Brain Box

Example: 
$$\begin{array}{r} 2\ 2 \\ +\ 1\ 5 \end{array}$$

Step 1: Add the numbers in the ones column
$$\begin{array}{r} 2\ 2 \\ +\ 1\ 5 \\ \hline 7 \end{array}$$

Step 2: Add the numbers in the tens column
$$\begin{array}{r} 2\ 2 \\ +\ 1\ 5 \\ \hline 3\ 7 \end{array}$$

The answer is **37**.

| | | |
|---|---|---|
| 21<br>+ 5 | 12<br>+ 13 | 23<br>+ 16 |
| 1<br>+ 6 | 10<br>+ 15 | 12<br>+ 7 |
| 10<br>+ 2 | 11<br>+ 14 | 18<br>+ 1 |

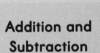

| | | |
|---|---|---|
| 13<br>+ 6 | 21<br>+ 4 | 22<br>+ 12 |
| 15<br>+ 23 | 14<br>+ 0 | 12<br>+ 34 |
| 20<br>+ 9 | 22<br>+ 7 | 28<br>+ 1 |

**Addition and Subtraction**

Adding single- and double-digit numbers

# Tic SubTract Toe

**Subtract** the numbers. To win tic-tac-toe, draw a line through the three answers that are the same.

|  |  |  |
|---|---|---|
| 19<br>− 5 | 25<br>− 4 | 38<br>− 26 |
| 15<br>− 2 | 26<br>− 13 | 28<br>− 15 |
| 27<br>− 5 | 28<br>− 11 | 30<br>− 10 |

**Addition and Subtraction**

|  |  |  |
|---|---|---|
| 21<br>− 10 | 28<br>− 2 | 18<br>− 4 |
| 29<br>− 11 | 15<br>− 4 | 31<br>− 21 |
| 25<br>− 20 | 27<br>− 1 | 23<br>− 12 |

# Brain Box

Example:    26<br>− 12

Step 1: Subtract the numbers in the ones column    26<br>− 12<br>4

Step 2: Subtract the numbers in the tens column    26<br>− 12<br>14

The answer is **14.**

185

| 19<br>−  3 | 28<br>− 12 | 17<br>−  1 |
|---|---|---|
| 23<br>− 10 | 35<br>− 24 | 26<br>−  5 |
| 30<br>− 10 | 19<br>−  8 | 23<br>− 21 |

| 27<br>− 20 | 26<br>− 14 | 19<br>−  8 |
|---|---|---|
| 19<br>− 12 | 36<br>− 16 | 24<br>−  1 |
| 38<br>− 31 | 17<br>− 16 | 27<br>− 11 |

**Addition and Subtraction**

Subtracting single- and double-digit numbers

# Colorful Math

**Add** or **subtract.**

Then use the key to color the spaces.

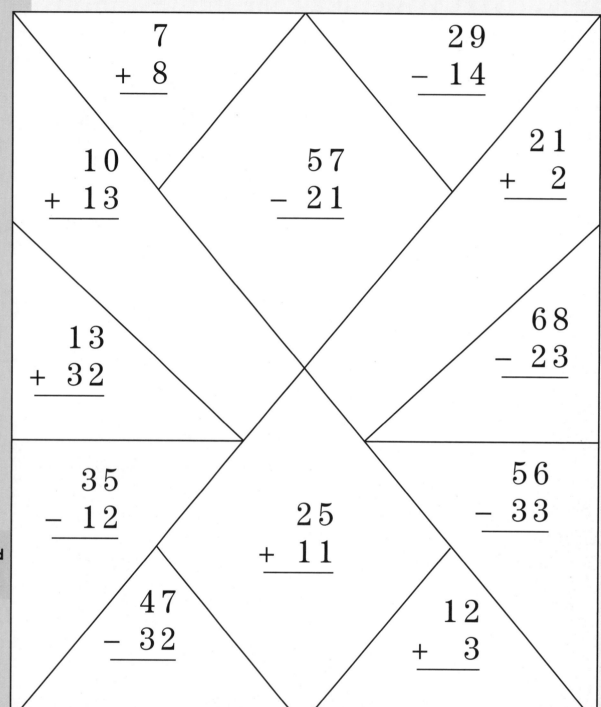

**Addition and Subtraction**

Addition and subtraction

| Answer | Color |
|--------|--------|
| 15 | Red |
| 23 | Blue |
| 36 | Yellow |
| 45 | Green |

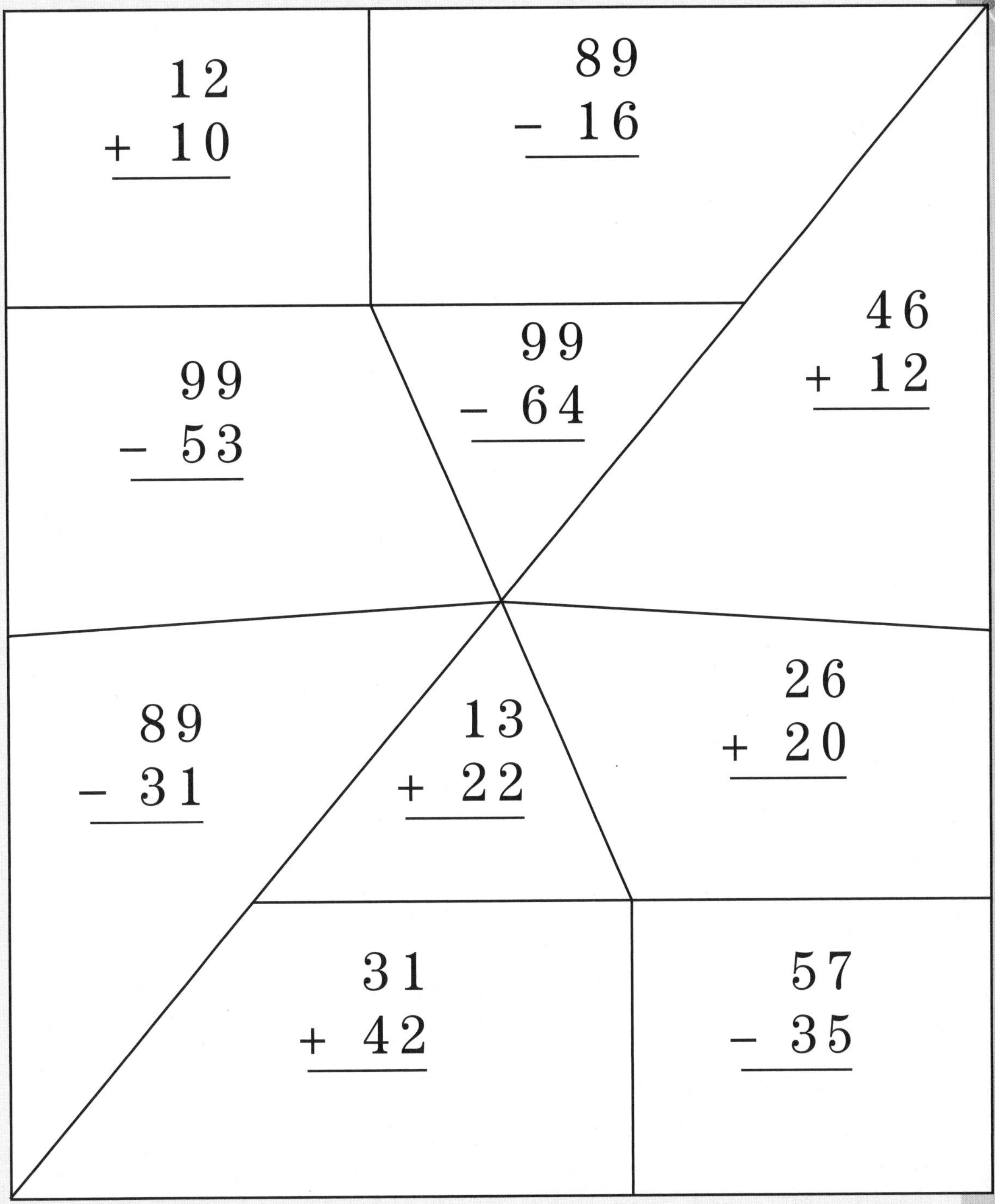

$$12 + 10$$

$$89 - 16$$

$$99 - 64$$

$$46 + 12$$

$$99 - 53$$

$$89 - 31$$

$$13 + 22$$

$$26 + 20$$

$$31 + 42$$

$$57 - 35$$

**Addition and Subtraction**

Addition and subtraction

| Answer | Color |
|---|---|
| 22 | Pink |
| 73 | Purple |
| 35 | Gray |
| 46 | Orange |
| 58 | Brown |

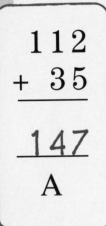

# Break the Code

Add or subtract.

```
  112
+  35
_____
  147
   A
```

```
  359
- 123
_____
   C
```

```
  242
+ 114
_____
   D
```

```
  987
- 556
_____
   E
```

```
  439
- 125
_____
   H
```

```
  171
+ 114
_____
   I
```

```
  223
+ 344
_____
   O
```

```
  587
- 114
_____
   V
```

Adding and subtracting three-digit numbers

**Addition and Subtraction**

# Brain Box

**Example:**

```
  321
+ 123
```

Step 1: Add the numbers in the ones column.

```
  3 2 1
+ 1 2 3
_____
      4
```

Step 2: Add the numbers in the tens column.

```
  3 2 1
+ 1 2 3
_____
    4 4
```

Step 3: Add the numbers in the hundreds column.

```
  3 2 1
+ 1 2 3
_____
  4 4 4
```

The answer is **444.**

Use your answers to decode the riddle.

Riddle:

What did one spy say to the other spy?

Answer:

___ ___ A ___ ___ A ___ ___ ___ ___
285  314 147 473 431 147 236 567 356 431

Adding and subtracting three-digit numbers

**Addition and Subtraction**

## Brain Box

**Example:**
```
  3 4 5
- 1 2 3
```

Step 1: Subtract the numbers in the ones column.
```
  3 4 5
- 1 2 3
      2
```

Step 2: Subtract the numbers in the tens column.
```
  3 4 5
- 1 2 3
    2 2
```

Step 3: Subtract the numbers in the hundreds column.
```
  3 4 5
- 1 2 3
  2 2 2
```

The answer is **222.**

# Math Riddle

**Add** or **subtract.**

```
  889
 -531
 ─────
   U
```

```
  263
 +135
 ─────
   C
```

```
  893
 -451
 ─────
   G
```

```
  244
 +125
 ─────
   E
```

```
  775
 -450
 ─────
   Y
```

```
  312
 +173
 ─────
   L
```

```
  222
 +345
 ─────
   H
```

```
  687
 -351
 ─────
   N
```

```
  764
 -651
 ─────
   I
```

**Addition and Subtraction**

Adding and subtracting three-digit numbers

```
  453
 +226
 ─────
   O
```

```
  241
 +151
 ─────
   R
```

```
  778
 -524
 ─────
   S
```

```
  551
 +132
 ─────
   T
```

Use your answers to decode the riddle.

## Riddle:

How can you tell if an elephant is under your bed?

## Answer:

___ ___ ___ ___    ___ ___ ___ ___
325  679  358  392    336  679  254  369

Addition and
Subtraction

Adding and
subtracting
three-digit
numbers

___ ___ ___ ___ ___ ___ ___    ___ ___ ___
683  679  358  398  567  369  254    683  567  369

___ ___ ___ ___ ___ ___ ___!
398  369  113  485  113  336  442

# Math Pun

Add the numbers using regrouping.

$$\begin{array}{r} {\scriptstyle 1} \\ 38 \\ +\ 8 \\ \hline \\ 46 \\ \hline \end{array}$$
A

$$\begin{array}{r} 15 \\ +38 \\ \hline \\ \hline \end{array}$$
S

$$\begin{array}{r} 54 \\ +18 \\ \hline \\ \hline \end{array}$$
T

$$\begin{array}{r} 31 \\ +19 \\ \hline \\ \hline \end{array}$$
I

$$\begin{array}{r} 26 \\ +\ 9 \\ \hline \\ \hline \end{array}$$
B

$$\begin{array}{r} 25 \\ +16 \\ \hline \\ \hline \end{array}$$
N

$$\begin{array}{r} 58 \\ +26 \\ \hline \\ \hline \end{array}$$
K

**Addition and Subtraction**

# Brain Box

**Example:**

$$\begin{array}{r} 2\ 8 \\ +\ 3\ 6 \\ \hline \end{array}$$

Sometimes you need to **regroup** numbers when you add.

When you add up the numbers in the ones column, the sum is **14**, which is one group of **10** and **4** ones.

Step 1. Write the **4** in the ones column and carry the 1 over to the top of the tens column.

$$\begin{array}{r} {\scriptstyle 1} \\ 2\ 8 \\ +\ 3\ 6 \\ \hline 4 \end{array}$$

Step 2. Then add up all the numbers—including the one you just added to the top—in the tens column.

$$\begin{array}{r} {\scriptstyle 1} \\ 2\ 8 \\ +\ 3\ 6 \\ \hline 6\ 4 \end{array}$$

The answer is **64**.

$$\begin{array}{r} 23 \\ +69 \\ \hline \phantom{00} \\ \end{array}$$
L

$$\begin{array}{r} 68 \\ +19 \\ \hline \phantom{00} \\ \end{array}$$
O

$$\begin{array}{r} 77 \\ +17 \\ \hline \phantom{00} \\ \end{array}$$
R

$$\begin{array}{r} 38 \\ +29 \\ \hline \phantom{00} \\ \end{array}$$
G

Use your answers to decode the riddle.

Riddle:

Where do dogs park their cars?

Answer:

___  ___     ___  ___  ___  ___  ___  ___  ___
50   41      35   46   94   84   50   41   67

___  ___  ___  ___
92   87   72   53

# 194

# Boat Bingo

Subtract using **regrouping.**
Color the cards with the answers that match the card on the right.

58

$$\begin{array}{r} \overset{5}{\cancel{6}}\overset{13}{\cancel{3}} \\ -\ 17 \\ \hline 46 \end{array}$$

$$\begin{array}{r} 55 \\ -\ 28 \\ \hline \end{array}$$

$$\begin{array}{r} 74 \\ -\ 59 \\ \hline \end{array}$$

$$\begin{array}{r} 92 \\ -\ 58 \\ \hline \end{array}$$

$$\begin{array}{r} 76 \\ -\ 18 \\ \hline \end{array}$$

$$\begin{array}{r} 90 \\ -\ 32 \\ \hline \end{array}$$

$$\begin{array}{r} 82 \\ -\ 59 \\ \hline \end{array}$$

$$\begin{array}{r} 70 \\ -\ 12 \\ \hline \end{array}$$

# Brain Box

Sometimes you need to **regroup** numbers to subtract.

**Example:**
$$\begin{array}{r} 3\ 2 \\ -\ 1\ 8 \\ \hline \end{array}$$

Step 1. Can you subtract **8** from **2**? No. So you'll have to **borrow** from the tens column. Remember, **32** is **3** groups of ten and **2** ones. Borrow **1** group of ten from the tens column so you can add ten ones to the ones column.

$$\begin{array}{r} \overset{2}{}\ \overset{12}{} \\ 3\ 2 \\ -\ 1\ 8 \\ \hline \end{array}$$

Step 2. Now you can subtract **8** from **12** in the ones column, which equals **4.**

$$\begin{array}{r} \overset{2}{}\ \overset{12}{} \\ 3\ 2 \\ -\ 1\ 8 \\ \hline 4 \end{array}$$

Step 3. In the tens column, you now have one less group of ten, so the 3 gets crossed out and becomes a 2. Now you can subtract **1** from **2** in the tens column, which equals **1.**

$$\begin{array}{r} \overset{2}{}\ \overset{12}{} \\ 3\ 2 \\ -\ 1\ 8 \\ \hline 1\ 4 \end{array}$$

The answer is **14.**

$$97 - 49$$

$$25 - 6$$

$$74 - 38$$

$$83 - 27$$

$$92 - 34$$

$$28 - 19$$

$$87 - 19$$

$$22 - 13$$

$$34 - 27$$

$$98 - 19$$

$$67 - 9$$

$$22 - 14$$

**Addition and Subtraction**

Subtraction with regrouping

$$73 - 15$$

$$43 - 34$$

$$58 - 29$$

$$33 - 29$$

# Hundreds of Gum Balls

Add the numbers using regrouping.

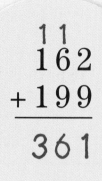

```
  1 1
  1 6 2
+ 1 9 9
-------
  3 6 1
```

```
  2 3 6
+ 1 8 5
-------
```

How many yellow
gum balls?

```
  2 6 5
+ 1 9 8
-------
```

How many
blue gum
balls?

How many red
gum balls?

Addition and
Subtraction

Adding
three-digit
numbers with
regrouping

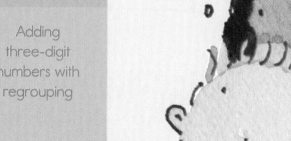

## Brain Box

Sometimes you need to **regroup** to add three-digit numbers.

Example:
$$\begin{array}{r} 2\,4\,6 \\ +\,3\,7\,9 \end{array}$$

First add the ones column. If the sum is more than 9, **regroup.** Carry the 1 to the tens column.

$$\begin{array}{r} \overset{1}{\phantom{0}}\phantom{00} \\ 2\,4\,6 \\ +\,3\,7\,9 \\ \hline \phantom{00}5 \end{array}$$

Next, add the tens column. If the sum is more than 9, **regroup.** Carry the 1 to the hundreds column.

$$\begin{array}{r} \overset{1}{\phantom{0}}\phantom{00} \\ 2\,4\,6 \\ +\,3\,7\,9 \\ \hline \phantom{0}2\,5 \end{array}$$

Now add the hundreds column.

$$\begin{array}{r} \overset{1}{\phantom{0}}\phantom{00} \\ 2\,4\,6 \\ +\,3\,7\,9 \\ \hline 6\,2\,5 \end{array}$$

The answer is **625.**

How many purple gum balls?

How many pink gum balls?

How many green gum balls?

$$\begin{array}{r} 2\,1\,7 \\ +\,2\,1\,7 \\ \hline \end{array}$$

$$\begin{array}{r} 2\,0\,9 \\ +\,2\,1\,2 \\ \hline \end{array}$$

$$\begin{array}{r} 1\,7\,7 \\ +\,2\,0\,6 \\ \hline \end{array}$$

**Addition and Subtraction**

Adding three-digit numbers with regrouping

# Aye, Aye, Captain!

Subtract using **regrouping**.

$$698 - 309$$

$$566 - 177$$

$$287 - 199$$

$$674 - 235$$

$$865 - 378$$

**Addition and Subtraction**

Subtracting three-digit numbers with regrouping

$$347 - 158$$

$$880 - 506$$

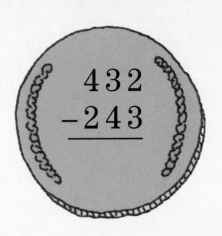

$$\begin{array}{r} 432 \\ -243 \\ \hline \end{array}$$

$$\begin{array}{r} 976 \\ -577 \\ \hline \end{array}$$

$$\begin{array}{r} 764 \\ -198 \\ \hline \end{array}$$

$$\begin{array}{r} 515 \\ -239 \\ \hline \end{array}$$

$$\begin{array}{r} 848 \\ -349 \\ \hline \end{array}$$

$$\begin{array}{r} 831 \\ -743 \\ \hline \end{array}$$

**Addition and Subtraction**

Subtracting three-digit numbers with regrouping

$$\begin{array}{r} 977 \\ -879 \\ \hline \end{array}$$

$$\begin{array}{r} 652 \\ -378 \\ \hline \end{array}$$

# Math Concentration

Add or subtract using **regrouping.**
Color the two cards with matching answers.

$$
\begin{array}{r}
236 \\
+145 \\
\hline
\end{array}
$$

$$
\begin{array}{r}
476 \\
-387 \\
\hline
\end{array}
$$

$$
\begin{array}{r}
943 \\
-136 \\
\hline
\end{array}
$$

$$
\begin{array}{r}
100 \\
-\ 88 \\
\hline
\end{array}
$$

$$
\begin{array}{r}
847 \\
+374 \\
\hline
\end{array}
$$

$$
\begin{array}{r}
673 \\
+328 \\
\hline
\end{array}
$$

**Addition and Subtraction**

Adding and subtracting three-digit numbers with regrouping

$$
\begin{array}{r}
701 \\
-689 \\
\hline
\end{array}
$$

$$
\begin{array}{r}
311 \\
+729 \\
\hline
\end{array}
$$

$$
\begin{array}{r}
669 \\
-288 \\
\hline
\end{array}
$$

# Multiplication and Fractions

# Times Fly

Finish the **addition** and **multiplication** sentences for each picture.

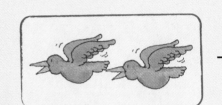 

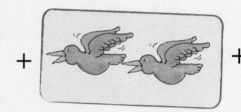 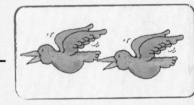

$$2 + 2 + \underline{\ 2\ } + \underline{\ 2\ } = \underline{\ 8\ }$$

$$2 \times 4 = \underline{\ 8\ }$$

**Multiplication and Fractions**

Addition and multiplication

 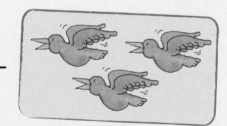

$$3 + \underline{\quad} + \underline{\quad} + \underline{\quad} + \underline{\quad} = \underline{\quad}$$

$$3 \times \underline{\quad} = \underline{\quad}$$

 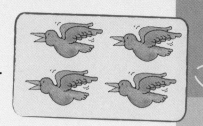

$4 + \underline{\hspace{1cm}} + \underline{\hspace{1cm}} = \underline{\hspace{1cm}}$

$4 \times \underline{\hspace{1cm}} = \underline{\hspace{1cm}}$

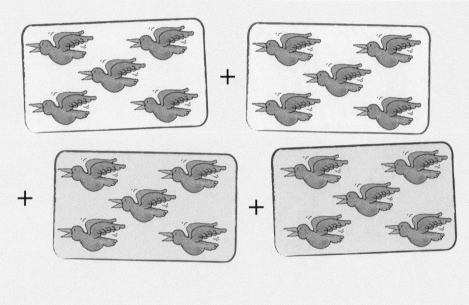

$5 + \underline{\hspace{1cm}} + \underline{\hspace{1cm}} + \underline{\hspace{1cm}} = \underline{\hspace{1cm}}$

$5 \times \underline{\hspace{1cm}} = \underline{\hspace{1cm}}$

**Multiplication and Fractions**

Addition and multiplication

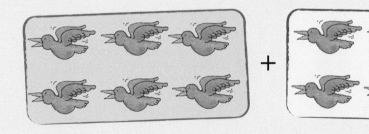

$6 + \underline{\hspace{1cm}} = \underline{\hspace{1cm}}$

$2 \times \underline{\hspace{1cm}} = \underline{\hspace{1cm}}$

203

# Harvest Times

### Finish the **addition sentences**.

$$5 \quad + \quad \boxed{\phantom{0}} \quad + \quad \boxed{\phantom{0}} \quad = \quad \boxed{\phantom{0}}$$

## Another way to write this sentence is like this:

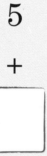

$$\begin{array}{c} 5 \\ + \\ \boxed{\phantom{0}} \\ + \\ \boxed{\phantom{0}} \\ \hline \boxed{\phantom{0}} \end{array}$$

**Multiplication and Fractions**

Addition and multiplication

## Brain Box

Math sentences can be written two ways:

$$2 + 3 = 5 \qquad \begin{array}{r} 2 \\ +\ 3 \\ \hline 5 \end{array} \qquad 3 \times 1 = 3 \qquad \begin{array}{r} 3 \\ \times\ 1 \\ \hline 3 \end{array}$$

Now write the same equation as a **multiplication sentence.**

$$5 \times \boxed{\phantom{0}} = \boxed{\phantom{0}}$$

Can you write the **multiplication sentence** the other way?

$$\begin{array}{r} 5 \\ \times\ \boxed{\phantom{0}} \\ \hline \boxed{\phantom{0}} \end{array}$$

Rewrite the **addition sentence** as a **multiplication sentence.**

$$6 + 6 + 6 = \boxed{\phantom{0}}$$

$$6 \times \boxed{\phantom{0}} = \boxed{\phantom{0}}$$

$$\begin{array}{r} 6 \\ \times\ \boxed{\phantom{0}} \\ \hline \boxed{\phantom{0}} \end{array}$$

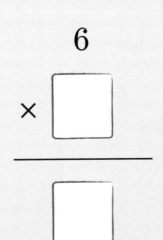

# Balloons!

Solve each problem.

Find the **multiplication** balloon that matches the **addition** balloon. Color it the same color.

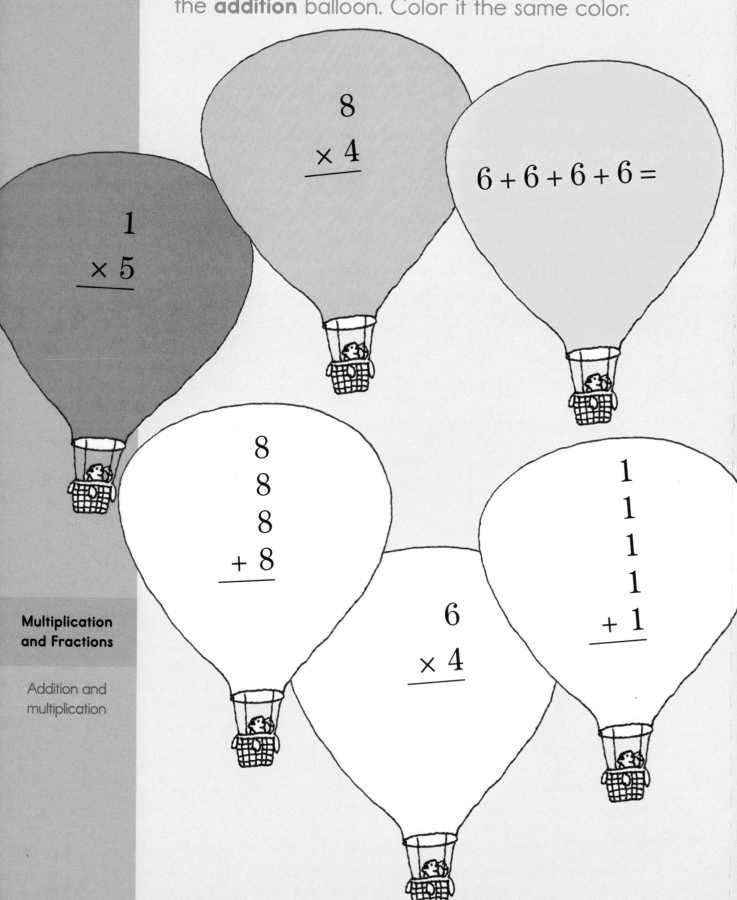

$$8 \times 4$$

$$6 + 6 + 6 + 6 =$$

$$1 \times 5$$

$$\begin{array}{r} 8 \\ 8 \\ 8 \\ + 8 \\ \hline \end{array}$$

$$6 \times 4$$

$$\begin{array}{r} 1 \\ 1 \\ 1 \\ + 1 \\ \hline \end{array}$$

# Time to Multiply

**Multiply.** Color each box yellow that equals less than 12.

| | | |
|---|---|---|
| $4 \times 4 =$ _____ | $3 \times 2 =$ _____ | $5 \times 4 =$ _____ |
| $5 \times 5 =$ _____ | $2 \times 2 =$ _____ | $3 \times 5 =$ _____ |
| $3 \times 3 =$ _____ | $4 \times 1 =$ _____ | $0 \times 5 =$ _____ |
| $2 \times 1 =$ _____ | $5 \times 2 =$ _____ | $8 \times 1 =$ _____ |
| $5 \times 3 =$ _____ | $2 \times 0 =$ _____ | $4 \times 5 =$ _____ |
| $4 \times 3 =$ _____ | $3 \times 3 =$ _____ | $3 \times 5 =$ _____ |

**Multiplication and Fractions**

Multiplication practice

What math symbol did you color? _____

What does the symbol tell you to do? _____

# Table Times 10

Write the missing numbers in the **times table.**

| × | 0 | 1 | 2 | 3 | 4 | 5 | 6 | 7 | 8 | 9 | 10 |
|---|---|---|---|---|---|---|---|---|---|---|----|
| **0** | 0 | 0 | 0 | 0 | 0 | 0 | 0 | 0 | 0 | 0 | 0 |
| **1** | 0 | 1 | 2 | 3 |   | 5 | 6 | 7 | 8 | 9 | 10 |
| **2** |   | 2 | 4 | 6 | 8 | 10 |   | 14 | 16 | 18 | 20 |
| **3** | 0 | 3 | 6 | 9 | 12 |   | 18 | 21 | 24 |   | 30 |
| **4** | 0 |   | 8 | 12 | 16 | 20 | 24 |   | 32 | 36 | 40 |
| **5** | 0 | 5 |   | 15 | 20 | 25 | 30 | 35 | 40 | 45 |   |
| **6** |   | 6 | 12 | 18 | 24 | 30 | 36 | 42 |   | 54 | 60 |
| **7** | 0 | 7 | 14 |   | 28 | 35 |   | 49 | 56 | 63 | 70 |
| **8** | 0 | 8 |   | 24 | 32 | 40 | 48 |   | 64 | 72 | 80 |
| **9** | 0 | 9 | 18 | 27 |   | 45 | 54 | 63 | 72 | 81 | 90 |
| **10** | 0 | 10 | 20 |   | 40 | 50 | 60 | 70 |   | 90 | 100 |

**Multiplication and Fractions**

# Brain Box

A **factor** is another word for a number in a multiplication equation.

A **product** is another word for the answer in a multiplication equation.

Example: 5 x 4 = 20

Both the **5** and the **4** are factors. **20** is the product.

Benito has 4 bags of marbles. There are 6 marbles in each bag. How many marbles does Benito have?

<u> 4 </u> × <u> 6 </u> = <u> 24 </u> marbles

Julia tied 1 balloon to the back of each chair. There are 8 chairs at the table. How many balloons does Julia need?

_____ × _____ = _____ balloons

Dad filled the washing machines with towels. Each machine holds 5 towels. Dad used 3 machines. How many towels did he wash?

_____ × _____ = _____ towels

Mom and Sis are hanging wallpaper. They have 3 rooms to do. Each room will need 9 rolls of wallpaper. How many rolls of wallpaper do they need to do all 3 rooms?

_____ × _____ = _____ rolls of wallpaper

**Multiplication and Fractions**

Times table and word problems

Each horse in the barn eats 3 buckets of oats every day. How many buckets of oats are needed to feed 4 horses?

_____ × _____ = _____ buckets

# ½ Equals One Half

Color **one half** of each shape.
Write the **fraction** in the space you colored.

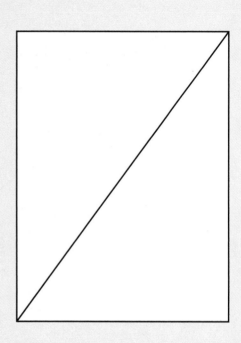

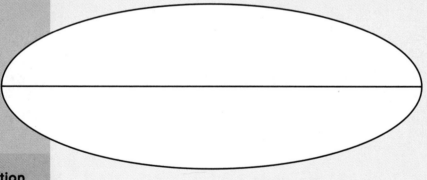

**Multiplication and Fractions**

Fractions

## Brain Box

**Fractions** show parts of a whole.

They can be written in words (**one half**) or as a figure ($\frac{1}{2}$).

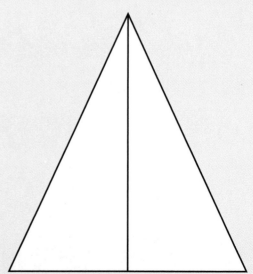

# $\frac{1}{4}$ Equals One Quarter

Color **one quarter** of each shape.
Write the **fraction** in the space you colored.

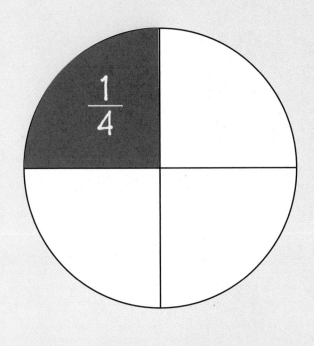

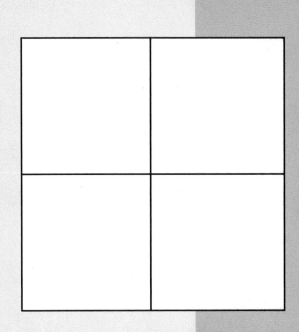

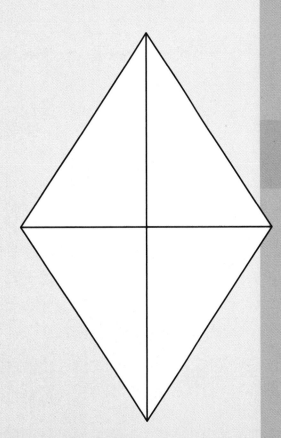

# $\frac{1}{3}$ Equals One Third

Color **one third** of each shape.
Write the **fraction** in the space you colored.

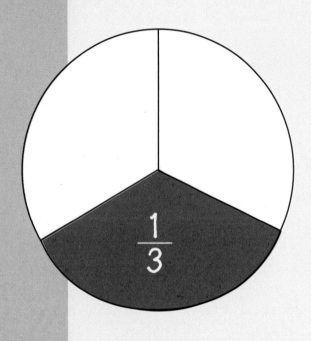

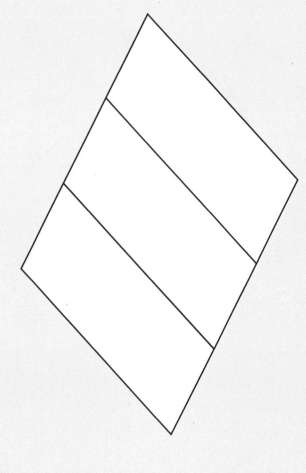

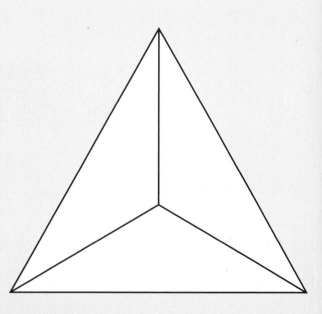

# A Piece of Pie

Draw a line from the **fraction** to the matching shape.

$$\frac{1}{2} \qquad \frac{1}{4} \qquad \frac{1}{3} \qquad \frac{2}{4} \qquad \frac{2}{6}$$

Color in the fractions below.

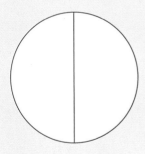

Color $\frac{1}{2}$ red.

Color $\frac{2}{3}$ blue.

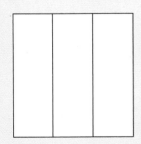

Color $\frac{1}{3}$ green.

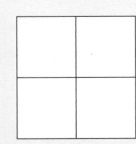

Color $\frac{1}{4}$ yellow.

**Multiplication and Fractions**

Matching fractions

# Word Problems

Read each problem.
Write the answer in words on the line.
Write the answer as a **fraction** in the box.

Ian cut his muffin in half. If he eats half of the muffin, how much will he have to give to his little brother?

_____  ☐

Fred's dog Daisy just had three puppies! One puppy is pure black. The other two are brown with little black spots. What fraction of the puppies are spotted?

_____  ☐

Dolores picked three yellow flowers and one pink flower. What fraction of the flowers are pink?

_____  ☐

# Shapes and Measurement

# Name That Shape!

Read the clues.
Write the names of the **shapes.**

 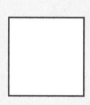 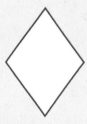 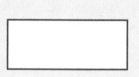 

I have four sides. Two of my sides are short. Two are long.

What am I? _____ rectangle _____

I have no sides at all. I go round and round.

What am I? _____

I have four sides. Each side is the same.

What am I? _____

I have four sides. You can find me in a deck of cards or on a baseball field.

What am I? _____

I have three sides.

What am I? _____

# Same Shape

Look at the shape on the top card.
Draw a matching shape on the card below.

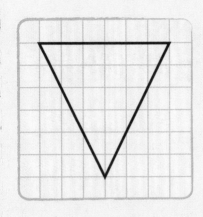

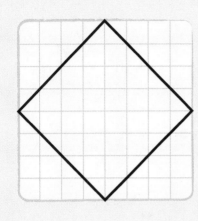

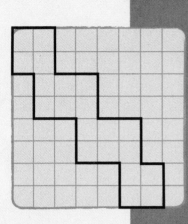

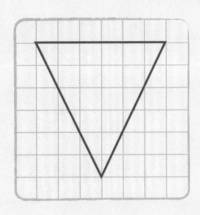

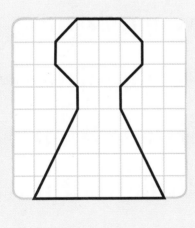

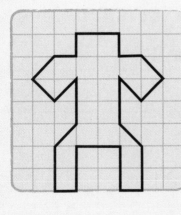

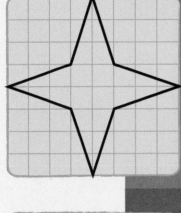

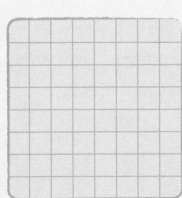

# Geometry Mystery

Read the clues.
Write the names of the shapes.

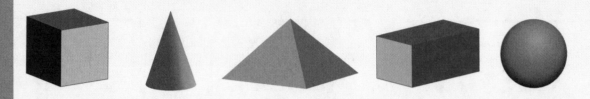

cube   cone   pyramid   box   sphere

I have a round bottom and a pointed top.

What am I? _____

I am round all over.

What am I? _____

I have four rectangular sides. I have two sides that are square.

What am I? _____

I have a square base and a pointed top.

What am I? _____

I have six square sides.

What am I? _____

# Measure It!

Circle the word that completes each sentence correctly.

Use a **scale** to measure height /(weight).

Use a **yardstick** to measure length / volume.

Use a **thermometer** to measure temperature / length.

Use a **measuring cup** to measure width / volume.

Write the **weight** of each basket of fruit.
Then answer the questions.

_____ pounds          _____ pounds

To measure the water in a swimming pool, would you use a cup or a gallon jug?

_____

To measure the distance from your room to the kitchen, would you use feet or miles?

_____

If the thermometer reads 35°F, would you wear a swimsuit or a snowsuit?

_____

# Inch by Inch

Cut out the **ruler** along the dotted line.
Use it to measure the pictures.
Then complete the sentences.
Save your ruler to use for the next five pages.

The quarter is __1__ inch wide.

The teaspoon is _____ inches long.

## Brain Box

To use your BRAIN QUEST ruler, put the red start edge at one end of the object you want to measure.

See where the end of the object lines up with the ruler. That number is your final measurement.

The toy car is _____ inches long.

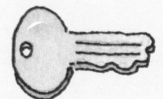

The key is _____ inches long.

**Shapes and Measurement**

Measuring with a ruler

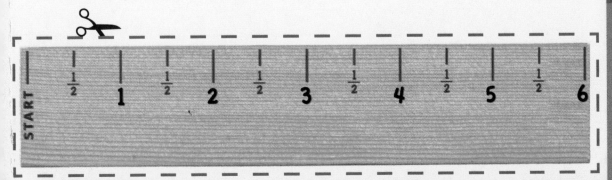

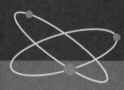

# Hand-y Measurements

Put one hand in the frame. Spread your fingers apart.
Use a pencil to trace around your fingers and hand.
Write which hand you traced on the frame.

My _____ Hand

**Shapes and Measurement**

Measuring with a ruler

Measure your hand with the ruler from page 221. Write the measurements to the nearest inch or half inch on the lines.

My hand is about _____ inches long.

My hand is about _____ inches wide.

My thumb is about _____ inches long.

My pointer finger is about _____ inches long.

My middle finger is about _____ inches long.

My ring finger is about _____ inches long.

My pinkie is about _____ inches long.

**Shapes and Measurement**

Measuring with a ruler

# My Little Piggies

Put one bare foot in the frame.
Try to spread your toes.
Use a pencil to trace around your foot.
Write which foot you traced on the frame.

My _____ Foot

Measure your foot with the ruler from page 221.
Write the measurements to the nearest inch or
half inch on the lines.

My foot is about _____ inches long.

My foot is about _____ inches wide.

My big toe is about _____ inches long.

My second toe is about _____ inches long.

My middle toe is about _____ inches long.

My fourth toe is about _____ inches long.

My little toe is about _____ inches long.

# The Right Size

Measure these things you can find in your home.

My favorite toy is _____ inches long.

My favorite book is _____ inches long

and _____ inches wide.

My favorite shoe is _____ inches long

and _____ inches wide.

The front door is _____ inches wide.

The kitchen counter is _____ inches long.

The kitchen sink is _____ inches deep.

My toothbrush is _____ inches long.

# Time
# and
# Money

# What Time Is It?

Find the two clocks that match the words.
Draw lines between the words
and the matching clocks.

## Brain Box

An analog clock
has three parts:

1. A clock face.

2. A little hand
that points to the
hour.

3. A big hand
that points to the
minute.

This clock says that it is
3 o'clock.

A digital clock
shows the time
in numbers:

This clock says it
is 3 o'clock, too.

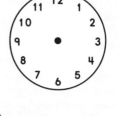

one o'clock

nine o'clock

ten o'clock

five o'clock

two o'clock

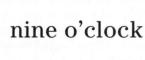

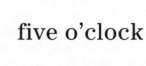

Add the missing hour hand to show the time.

2:00

10:00

5:00

7:00

# Half Past

Color the clocks that show **half past** the hour.

## Brain Box

One hour equals **60** minutes.

Half an hour equals **30** minutes.

Look at this clock:

The big hand is pointing to the **6.** This means it's **30** minutes after the hour, or **half past** the hour.

This clock says it's half past **12,** or **12:30.**

Add the missing minute hand to show the time.

**5:30**    **7:30**    **1:30**    **4:30**

**Time and Money**

Half hours

# 15 Minutes Before and After

## Brain Box

A quarter hour is **15** minutes.

Look at this clock:

The big hand is pointing to the **3**. This means it's **15** minutes after the hour, or a **quarter past.**

The clock says it's a quarter past **1** or **1:15.**

Now look at this clock:

The big hand is pointing to the **9.** This means it's **45** minutes after the hour, or **12:45.**

It also means that it is **15** minutes to the next hour, or a **quarter to** the hour.

**Time and Money**

Quarter hours

Find the clock faces that show a **quarter past** the hour. Color them yellow.

Find the clock faces that show a **quarter to** the hour. Color them blue.

Add the missing minute hand to show the time.

**12:15**      **11:45**      **5:45**      **8:15**

# It's Getting Late!

Add the clock hands to show one hour later.
Write the new time on the line.

**1:00**    **2:00**    **3:00**    _____

**5:00**    _____    **7:00**    _____

What time is it right now?
Write the time on the line.
Add the clock hands.

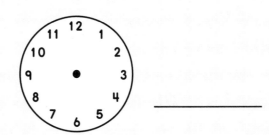 _____

What time will it be in
an hour?
Write the time on the line.
Add the clock hands.

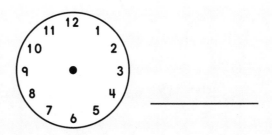 _____

Brain Quest Second Grade Workbook

# My Times

Write the time on the **digital** clock.
Then add the clock hands to show
the same time on the **analog** clock.

I wake up at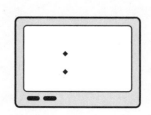

I go to school at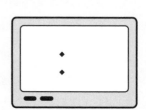

I come home at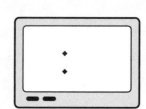

I eat dinner at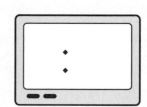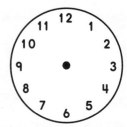

**Time and Money**

Daily schedule

I go to bed at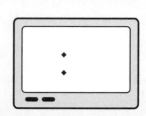

# Tell the Time

Write the time below each clock.

**12:45** _____   _____   _____

_____   _____   _____   _____

_____   _____   _____   _____

_____   _____   _____   _____

**Time and Money**

Telling time

# Money Riddles

Read the clues and questions.
Circle the answers.

## Brain Box

penny

nickel

dime

quarter

I am worth 5 pennies.
Two of me make a dime.
What am I?

How many cents am I worth?

1¢          5¢          10¢          25¢

. . . . . . . . . . . . . . . . . . . . . . . . . . . . . . . . . . . . . . . . .

I am the smallest coin. But I am worth
more than a nickel or a penny.
What am I?

How many cents am I worth?

1¢          5¢          10¢          25¢

**Time and Money**

Penny, nickel, dime, quarter

I am not silver. You need 100 of
me to make a dollar.
What am I?

How many cents am I worth?

1¢          5¢          10¢          25¢          100¢

I am one-fourth of a dollar. I am worth
5 nickels or 2 dimes and 5 pennies.
What am I?

How many cents am I worth?

1¢          5¢          10¢          25¢

Time and
Money

Penny, nickel,
dime, quarter

# Toy Store

Circle the exact change needed to buy each toy.
Then count the change left over.

56¢

How much money is left? _____28¢_____

87¢

How much money is left? _____

92¢

How much money is left? _____

How much money is left? _____

Count the money.

How much more money would you need to

buy the toy? _____

What coins would make up that amount?

_____

_____

# Got Change?

How many of each coin equal a **dollar?**
Write the missing numbers in the chart.

## Brain Box

This is a dollar bill.

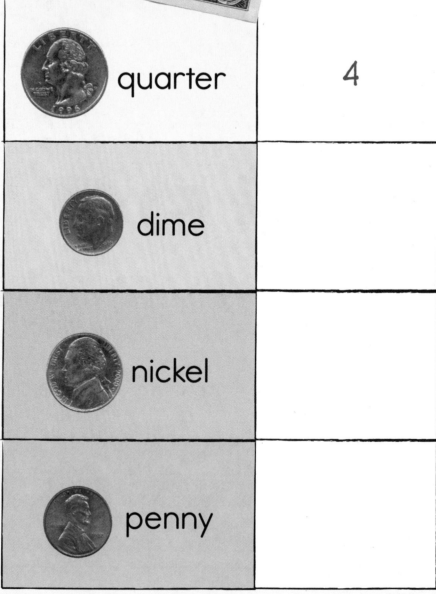

| | |
|---|---|
| quarter | 4 |
| dime | |
| nickel | |
| penny | |

# Even Steven

How many equal the same amount of money?

 = _____5_____ ×

 = _____ ×

 = _____ ×

 = _____ ×

 = _____ ×

# Which Is More?

Add the coins.

Write the amount on the line.

Compare the coins to the dollar bill or bills.

Circle the **greater** amount.

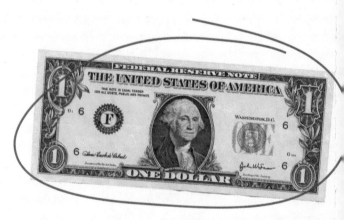

Total  85¢

Total _____

241

Total _____

Adding money

Total _____

# Piggy Bank

Draw a line from each group of coins to the matching piggy bank.

# Social Studies

# Who's the Boss?

Read about bosses.

A boss keeps your school, town, state, or country safe and running smoothly. Some bosses are hired. Teachers and principals are hired to teach and run schools.

Some bosses are elected. These bosses are usually called leaders. American citizens who are at least 18 years old can vote. Americans who think they would make good leaders run for office. Voters vote for the person they think will do the best job.

The boss of your city or town is the mayor. The mayor is the city's highest elected official. The boss of your state is the governor. The governor is the state's highest elected official. The boss of the country is the president. The president is the most important leader in the United States.

## Who's the boss of your classroom?

_____
**your teacher's name**

## Who's the boss of your school?

_____
**your principal's name**

Answer the questions.
Then tape or glue pictures of your leaders in the boxes below.

Who is the boss of your city or town?

The mayor of

_____
your city/town

is _____ .

Who is the boss of your state?

The governor of

_____
your state

is _____ .

Who is the boss of the United States?

The President of the United States is

_____ .

**Social Studies**

Important
leaders

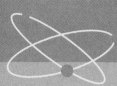
# State Capitals

Use the map that comes with this workbook to help you fill in the **state capitals.**

Montgomery
Alabama

Alaska

Arizona

Arkansas

California

Colorado

Connecticut

Delaware

Florida

Georgia

Hawaii

Idaho

Illinois

Indiana

Iowa

Kansas

Kentucky

Louisiana

Maine

Maryland

Massachusetts

Michigan

Minnesota

Mississippi

Missouri

Montana

Nebraska

Nevada

New Hampshire

New Jersey

New Mexico

New York

North Carolina

North Dakota

Ohio

Oklahoma

Oregon

Pennsylvania

Rhode Island

South Carolina

South Dakota

Tennessee

Texas

Utah

Vermont

Virginia

Washington

West Virginia

Wisconsin

Wyoming

What is the capital of the country?

Social Studies

State capitals

# Map It!

Use the **map key** to label the continents.

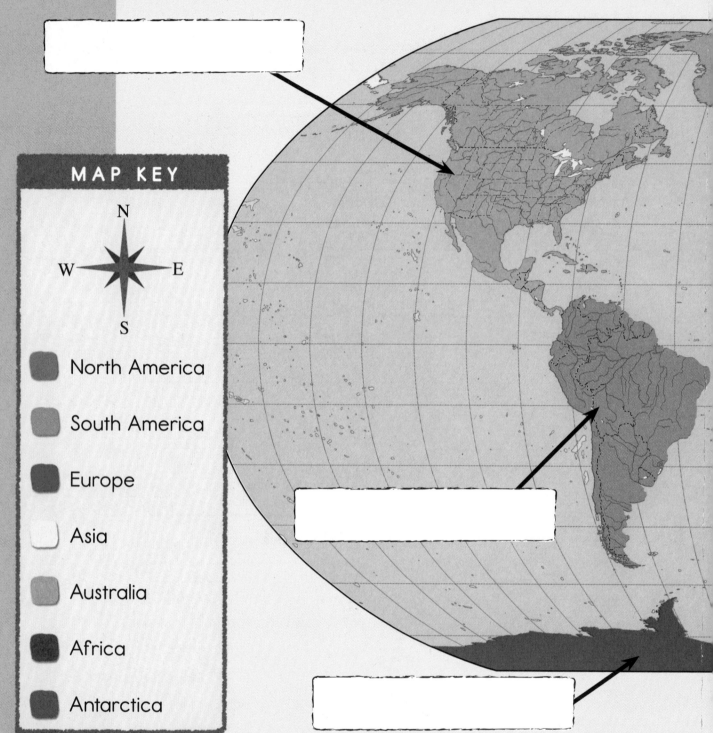

**MAP KEY**

N
W ✦ E
S

🟦 North America

🟦 South America

🟦 Europe

⬜ Asia

🟦 Australia

🟦 Africa

🟦 Antarctica

---

## Brain Box

A **map** of the world is a picture of the Earth's surface.

A **compass** shows the four directions: **N**orth, **S**outh, **E**ast, **W**est.

A **key** or **legend** explains the small pictures or symbols on the map.

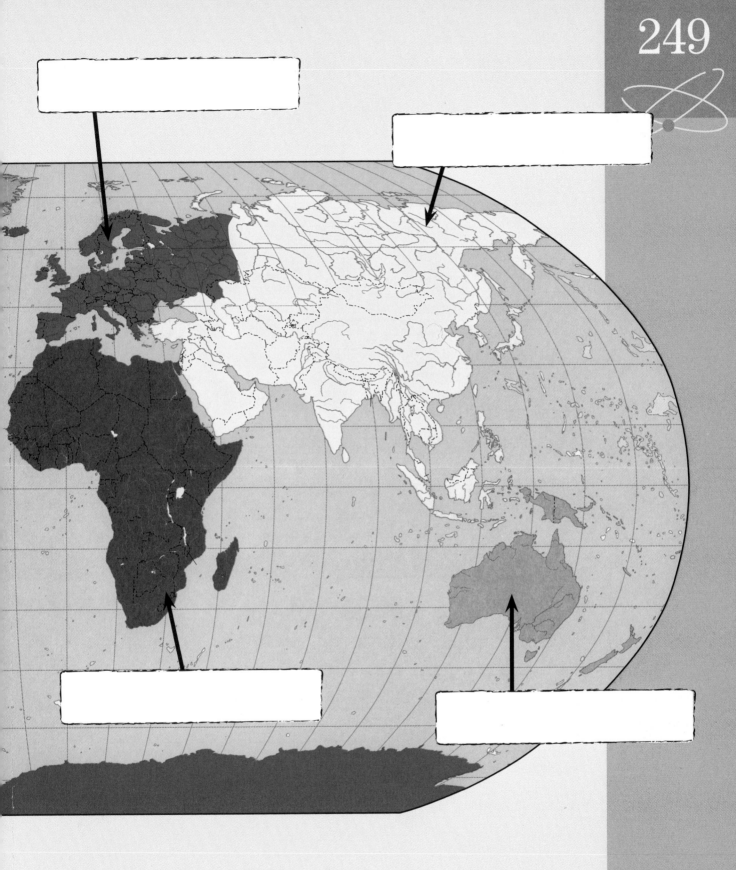

Is Europe north or south of Africa? _____

Is Africa east or west of Australia? _____

Is Antarctica west or south of Asia? _____

# Following Directions

Use the **map** on the next page to complete the sentences.

All the kids start at school.

I am going 4 blocks north and 1 block east.

Josh is going to the

_____ .

I am going 2 blocks south and 2 blocks west.

Jen is going to the

_____ .

I am going 2 blocks south and 2 blocks east.

Jane is going to the _____ .

I am going 1 block north and 3 blocks east.

Jeremy is going to the

_____ .

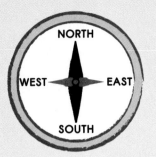

| | | | | music school | | |
|---|---|---|---|---|---|---|
| post office | | | | | | |
| | | | | | | |
| | | | | | | library |
| | | | school | | | |
| | | | | | | |
| | ball field | | | | market | |
| | | | | | | |
| | play-ground | | | | | |

# The Lady in the Harbor

Read about the Statue of Liberty.

The **crown** with seven **spikes** stands for the seven seas and the seven continents.

The **torch** is a light that welcomes travelers to the United States.

JULY IV

The **tablet** shows the Roman numerals of the date the Declaration of Independence was signed: July 4, 1776.

The **foot's forward position** is a symbol of moving forward into the future.

The Statue of Liberty stands on an island in New York Harbor. She is a symbol of freedom and hope.

Write a poem about what liberty means to you.
Begin the first word of each line with the
letter shown.

L_____

I_____

B_____

E_____

R_____

T_____

Y_____

Draw a picture for your poem.

**Social Studies**

National
monument

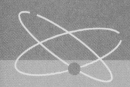

# Calendar Crunch

Write the months of the year in order on the **time line.**

Use the words in the box.

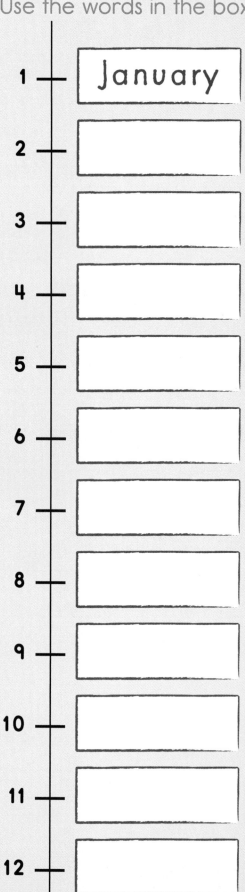

1 — January

2 —

3 —

4 —

5 —

6 —

7 —

8 —

9 —

10 —

11 —

12 —

| April |
| August |
| December |
| February |
| January |
| July |
| June |
| March |
| May |
| November |
| October |
| September |

List all the birthdays and holidays you celebrate on the calendar.

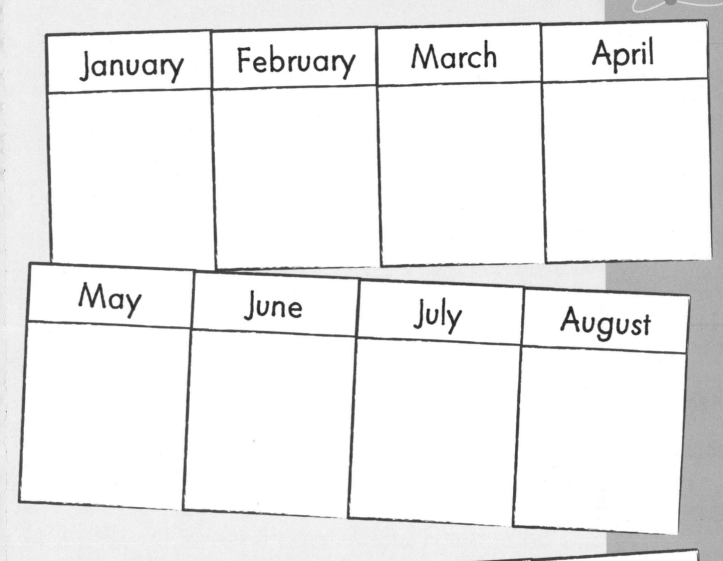

| January | February | March | April |
|---|---|---|---|
| | | | |

| May | June | July | August |
|---|---|---|---|
| | | | |

| September | October | November | December |
|---|---|---|---|
| | | | |

# Spreading the Word!

There are many ways to communicate.
Some are old, some are no longer used,
and some are new.

## Long ago

Long ago, if you wanted to invite friends
to your party, you would go over to
their house and deliver the invitation **by
hand** . . . or send an invitation **in the mail.**

## 1840s

Starting in 1843, you could send your
invitation **by telegraph.** The telegraph used
Morse code to send messages. Morse code
is an alphabet of dots and dashes that stand
for individual letters. Telegraph operators
translated Morse code into words.

## 1860s

Long before Federal Express, there was the **Pony Express.** The
Pony Express was a special mail service that began in April 1860
and ended in October 1861. Brave riders rode their horses from St.
Joseph, Missouri, to Sacramento, California. If you and your friends
lived along the route, you could send an invitation by Pony Express.

## 1900s

By the early 1900s, you could
**telephone** friends to invite
them to your party. Alexander
Graham Bell invented the
telephone in 1876.

## Today

Now you can use a **cell phone** to
tell your friends about your party
with a call, text, or photo. The first
cell phone call was made in 1975.

**Social Studies**

Past, present,
future

Fill in the blanks on the **time line.**

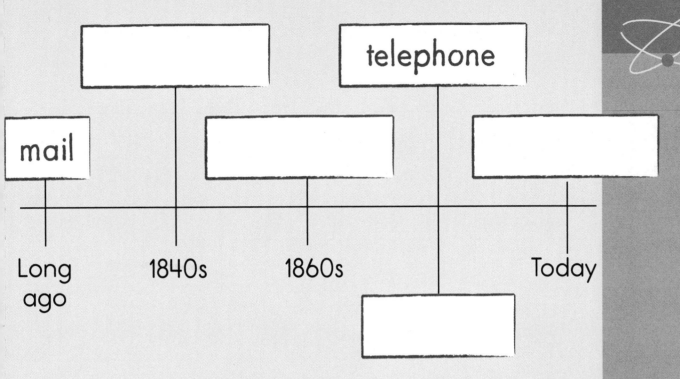

How do you think people will communicate in the future?

Describe and draw your "communication invention" of the future.

Past, present, future

Martin Luther
King Day

# I Have a Dream

Read about Martin Luther King Jr.

Martin Luther King Jr. was a great civil rights leader. A civil rights leader works toward making the world a place where all people are treated fairly. Dr. King made speeches and organized marches to spread his message. In 1963, he gave his famous "I Have a Dream" speech at a huge rally for civil rights in Washington, D.C.

Here is part of it:

"I have a dream . . . a dream that my four little children will one day live in a nation where they will not be judged by the color of their skin but by the content of their character."

**Social Studies**

Dr. King's birthday is celebrated across the United States on the third Monday in January.

Do you have a dream for the United States? Write your own "I Have a Dream" speech on the lines below.

I have a dream that _____

_____

_____

_____

_____

_____

_____

# Big Birthdays

Read about George Washington and Abraham Lincoln.

George Washington and Abraham Lincoln were born in the month of February. Both presidents have monuments in our nation's capital, Washington, D.C. Each year, we celebrate their lives and achievements on Presidents Day, the third Monday in February.

George Washington was the first President of the United States, from 1789 to 1797. He was born February 22, 1732, in Virginia. The Washington Monument honors Washington's life. It is a tall stone obelisk. An obelisk is a four-sided stone tower. Inside, 897 steps take visitors to a room near the top. What a view!

Abraham Lincoln was the 16th President of the United States, from 1861 to 1865. He was born February 12, 1809, in Kentucky. The Lincoln Memorial looks like a Greek temple. It is a building with three rooms. A statue of Abraham Lincoln sits in the center room.

**Washington Monument**

**Lincoln Memorial**

**Social Studies**

Presidents Day

## Across

2. The Lincoln _ _ _ _ _ _ _ _ has three rooms.

4. The national holiday celebrated on the third Monday in February is

_ _ _ _ _ _ _ _ _ _ Day.

6. The Washington _ _ _ _ _ _ _ _ is a tall tower.

## Down

1. George Washington was the

_ _ _ _ _ president.

3. Washington, D.C., is the _ _ _ _ _ _ _ of the United States.

5. The 16th president was Abraham

_ _ _ _ _ _ _ .

# Big Birthdays

Read about the Fourth of July.

We celebrate America's birthday on the fourth day of July. The Fourth of July is also called Independence Day.

On July 4, 1776, the Continental Congress met in Philadelphia, Pennsylvania, and adopted the Declaration of Independence. This paper said that America was no longer ruled by England. It declared America free! The Declaration is still a symbol of American liberty. We celebrate what it stands for every Fourth of July.

We celebrate this holiday in many different ways.
To find out how, unscramble each word.

FIOKWERSR   _fireworks_

LGAF   _ _ _ _

TCONREC   _ _ _ _ _ _ _

PRADEA   _ _ _ _ _ _

# Turkey Day!

Read about Thanksgiving.

We celebrate Thanksgiving on the fourth Thursday in November.

In 1621, the Pilgrims celebrated their colony's first successful harvest with the Native American Wampanoag tribe. We continue this tradition of giving thanks by celebrating Thanksgiving.

The Pilgrims were thankful for their harvest.
What are **you** thankful for? Write about it below.

_____

_____

_____

_____

**Social Studies**

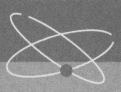

# American Women

Read about these important American women.
Write their names and birthdays on the
**time line** below.

## AMELIA EARHART (born 1897)

In 1932, Amelia Earhart became the first
female aviator to fly across the Atlantic Ocean
alone. Her flight set a new world record. She
made it across in 13 hours and 30 minutes.
Earhart showed that women were strong and as brave as men.

## SACAGAWEA (born 1788)

Sacagawea was a Shoshone Native
American woman. She was a member
of the Lewis and Clark Expedition from
1805 to 1806. She helped Lewis and
Clark explore the western part of the United States.

## SOJOURNER TRUTH (born 1797)

Sojourner Truth was an African-
American woman who worked to end
slavery and improve women's rights.
Born into slavery, she escaped later in
her life and lived as a free woman.

Sacagawea, 1788

| 1780 | 1800 | | 1850 |

## ROSA PARKS (born 1913)

Rosa Parks was an African-American who worked for civil rights. In 1955, in Montgomery, Alabama, she refused to give up her bus seat to a white man. She was arrested because of this, and became a symbol of bravery and protest.

## ELEANOR ROOSEVELT (born 1884)

Eleanor Roosevelt worked toward making the world a place where all people are treated equally. She was the wife of President Franklin Delano Roosevelt. She represented the President around the country, and was the U.S. representative to the United Nations.

## SUSAN B. ANTHONY (born 1820)

Susan B. Anthony worked to get equal rights for women. She led protests so that women would be allowed to speak in public, own property, and have the right to vote.

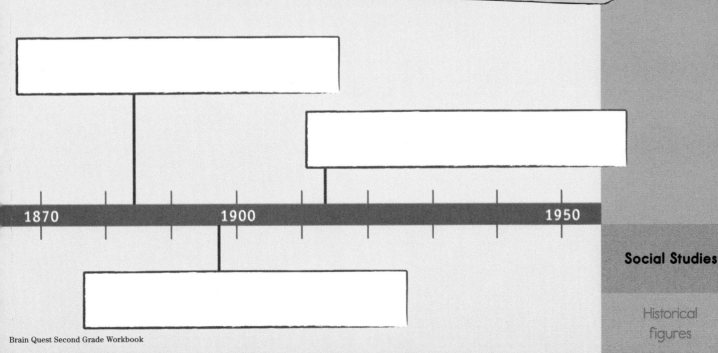

1870            1900            1950

**Social Studies**

Historical figures

# American Men

Read about these important American men.
Write their names and birthdays on the
**time line** below.

## PAUL REVERE (born 1735)

Paul Revere was an important American patriot.
He was an ordinary man who worked as a
silversmith. But one night in 1775, he rode from
Boston toward Concord, Massachusetts, to warn the Americans
there that British troops were coming. This act of bravery helped
America win her independence.

## THOMAS EDISON (born 1847)

Thomas Edison was one of the greatest
inventors of all time. He invented more than
1,000 different things, including the electric
light and the movie camera. His inventions forever
changed the way people work and play.

## THURGOOD MARSHALL (born 1908)

Thurgood Marshall was the first African-American
justice on the U.S. Supreme Court. He began his career
as a civil rights lawyer. In 1954 he won a case called
*Brown v. Board of Education*. This made segregation
illegal, and paved the way for the civil rights movement in America.

Paul Revere, 1735

1700   1750   1800   1850

**Social Studies**

Historical
figures

## JACKIE ROBINSON (born 1919)

Jackie Robinson was the first African-American to play on a major league baseball team. By breaking the color barrier, he led the way for all the great African-American athletes that came after him.

## ORVILLE WRIGHT (born 1871)
## WILBUR WRIGHT (born 1867)

The Wright brothers were the coinventors of the airplane. On December 17, 1903, Orville flew the plane above the sand dunes of Kitty Hawk, North Carolina. Although he flew only 120 feet and the flight lasted just 12 seconds, it marked the beginning of a new age of air travel.

## CESAR CHAVEZ (born 1927)

Cesar Chavez was a Mexican-American union leader. A union leader helps organize workers to stand up to their bosses for fair treatment and fair pay. In 1962, with Dolores Huerta, Chavez started a union called the United Farm Workers of America. His work led to better conditions and pay for migrant workers.

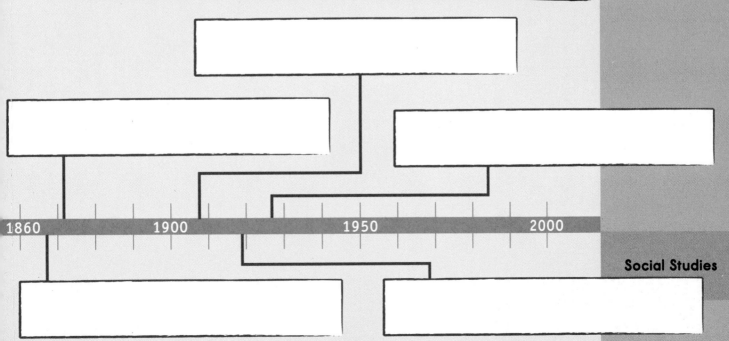

1860       1900        1950        2000

**Social Studies**

Brain Quest Second Grade Workbook

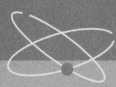

# My Time Line!

Fill in the **time line** starting with the year you were born. Then, imagine your future and fill in all the key events of your life!

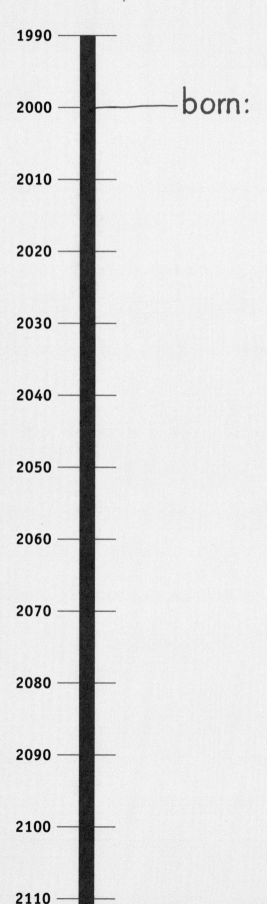

1990

2000 —— born:

2010

2020

2030

2040

2050

2060

2070

2080

2090

2100

2110

# Science

# What Am I?

Read the riddles.
Answer each riddle with a
word from the Word Box.

| gold | turtle |
|--------|--------|
| potato | coal |
| snail | carrot |

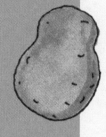

I grow underground.

French fries are made of me.

What am I? _____ **potato** _____

I hatch from an egg, but I have no feathers. I carry
my home with me. When I'm scared, I pull my
head and four legs inside my shell.

What am I? _____

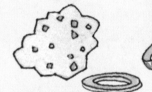

# Brain Box

An **animal** is a living creature.

A **vegetable** is a plant that
people and animals can eat.

A **mineral** is found in rocks
and in the ground.

I'm found in rocks underground. I'm a
shiny yellow color. I make a pretty ring
or necklace.

What am I? _____

I'm orange. Rabbits find me very yummy!

What am I? _____

Categories

**Science**

I travel very slowly inch by inch.

What am I? _____

I can be used for fuel.

What am I? _____

Write each word from the Word Box under the correct heading in the chart. Then add one of your own words to each column.

| Animals | Vegetables | Minerals |
|---------|------------|----------|
|         |            |          |

Categories

**Science**

Brain Quest Second Grade Workbook

# Water Goes Round

Read about the **water cycle.**

Sun shines on the sea and on rivers, lakes, and ponds.

Water from the rain runs into the sea and into rivers, lakes, and ponds. Then the cycle begins again.

The water evaporates and becomes part of the air. Water in the air is called water vapor. The warm water vapor rises. The higher it goes, the cooler it gets.

When water vapor cools, it forms clouds. Rain falls from the clouds.

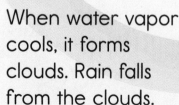

Label each picture with a phrase from the box.

| rain falls | clouds form |
| --- | --- |
| water vapor rises | sun shines |

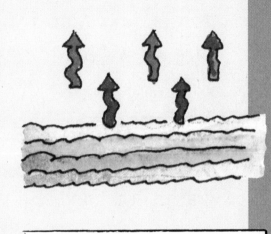

The water cycle

**Science**

Brain Quest Second Grade Workbook

# Water Everywhere!

Read about **water**.

### Liquid

Water is a liquid. Liquid water is wet. Rivers, ponds, lakes, and the sea have liquid water. Clouds are made of tiny water droplets.

### Gas

Water is a gas. The gas form is called water vapor. Water vapor is part of the air. When the air feels damp or moist, the air has lots of water vapor in it. Steam is hot water vapor. Fog is cool water vapor.

### Solid

Solid water is ice. A snowflake is made up of ice crystals. Ice cubes and icebergs are water in solid form.

Write **liquid, gas,** or **solid** under each picture.

_____

_____

_____

_____

_____

_____

# Energy to Grow

Read about **photosynthesis.**

You need energy to play. You get your energy from the food you eat. Plants need energy to grow, too. Plants get the energy they need from sunlight. Plants use air, water, and sunlight to make their own food. A green substance in plants called chlorophyll [KLOR-uh-fil] absorbs sunlight and makes plants green. Inside plants, the chlorophyll uses the light energy and air to make the food they need to grow. This process is called photosynthesis [foh-toh-sin-thuh-sis].

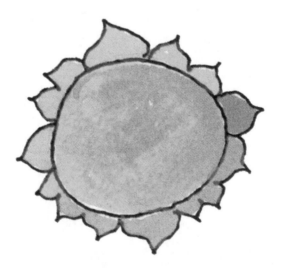

Read about the experiment.
Number the pictures to show the
correct order of the steps.

1. A plant uses
   sunlight to
   make food.
   A healthy
   plant is green.

2. Cover one
   leaf with foil.

3. After five
   days, uncover
   the leaf.

Complete the sentence.

The leaf turned yellow because it didn't get the

_____ it needed

to make it green.

Photosynthesis

**Science**

# Light

Read about **light.**

Is light white? No! Light is made up of colors. When light passes through raindrops, high above the earth, the light rays bend. When light bends, we see the colors of the rainbow.

What are the colors of the rainbow? You can remember the colors of the rainbow in order by remembering the name "ROY G. BIV." Red is usually on the outside part of the rainbow; violet is usually on the inside part.

R for red
O for orange
Y for yellow
G for green
B for blue
I for indigo
V for violet

Color the rainbow.

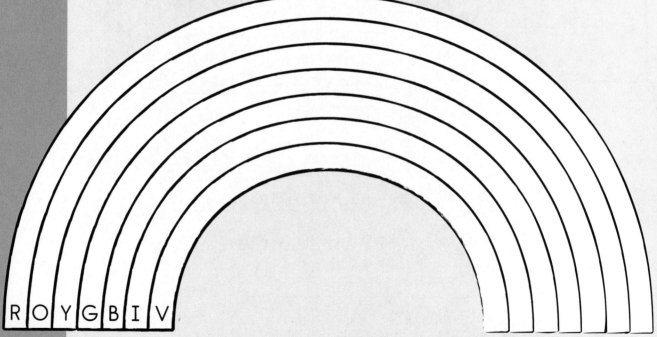

R O Y G B I V

Rainbows

**Science**

# Moonlight

Read about the **moon.**

The moon goes through phases as it travels around the Earth. The shapes of the phases are the parts of the moon lit by the sun.

A **full** moon is round like a circle.

A **gibbous** moon is larger than a half moon.

A **half** moon is half a circle.

A **crescent** moon looks like a sideways smile. It is smaller than a half moon.

A **new** moon is not visible because the side of the moon facing the Earth gets no sunlight.

Label the phases of the moon.

full

**What kind of moon do you see tonight?**

_____

Phases of the moon

**Science**

You live in a home on a street or road.

Your street or road is in a town or city.

Your town or city is in a state.

Your state is in a country.

Your country is on a continent.

Your continent is on the planet Earth.

And where is the Earth?

The Earth is in the solar system. It is one of eight planets in our solar system that orbit around the sun. Pluto was once considered a planet, but scientists have decided that it's too small to be considered a full planet. Pluto is now called a dwarf planet.

Circle the **Earth** in the picture below.
Use the picture to answer the questions.

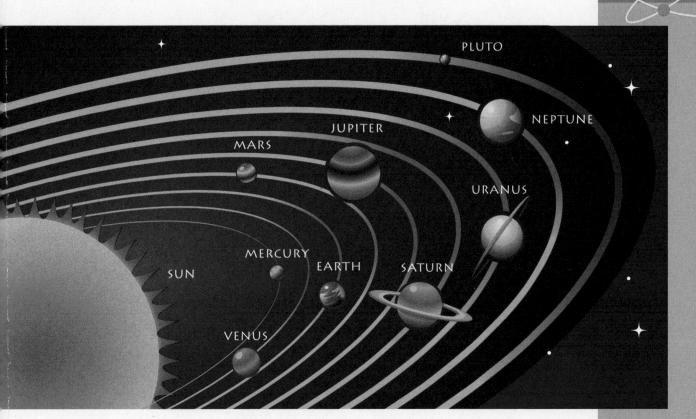

What is the largest planet in the solar system?

_____.

What two planets have rings?

_____.

List the eight planets that orbit around the sun.

_____.

_____.

What type of planet is Pluto?

_____.

Our solar
system

Science

# Stay Healthy!

Maiko loves to jump rope to stay healthy.

She made a **chart** to keep track of how long she jumps rope each day.

Use her chart to answer the questions.

| CHART | |
| --- | --- |
| **Day** | **Minutes** |
| Mon. | 15 |
| Tues. | 10 |
| Wed. | 20 |
| Thurs. | 12 |
| Fri. | 18 |
| Sat. | 18 |
| Sun. | 13 |

On which day did Maiko exercise the most?

_____

On which day did she exercise the least?

_____

On which two days did she exercise the same amount of time?

_____

Use the **chart** to complete the **graph** for Thursday through Sunday.

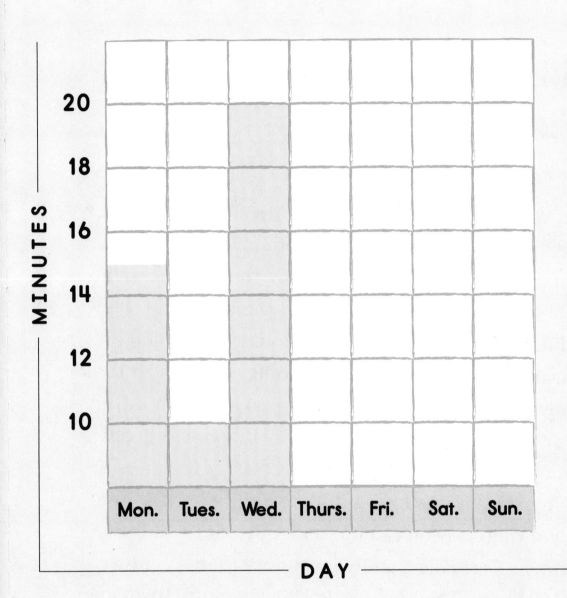

How do **you** exercise to keep your heart and

lungs healthy? _____

_____

# The Hippo and the Tortoise

Read the story.

## This is not a fable. It is a true story.

In 2004, there was a deadly storm. The rain swept a baby hippo away from his mother. The hippo was less than a year old. The rain took the baby down a river in Kenya. The river washed the hippo into the Indian Ocean. He weighed 650 pounds. Then huge storm waves left the hippo standing on a reef. It took many boats, ropes, nets, and cars to save him. After he was brought to shore, the baby hippo was given the name Owen.

Then Owen was brought to a wildlife park. When he got there, Owen ran up to an old giant male tortoise. Tortoises can live for more than a century, or 100 years. This tortoise is 130 years old. His name is Mzee. Now Owen and Mzee swim, eat, and sleep side by side. Owen follows Mzee the same way he would have followed his mother. Hippos stay with their moms for about four years. Now Owen has a new "mother."

Nonfiction

**Science**

| Kenya |
| oceans |
| fable |
| rough |
| years |

Use words from the Word Box to complete the sentences.

This story is not a __ __ __ __ __ .

The waves were __ __ __ __ __ .

Atlantic, Pacific, and Indian are names of

__ __ __ __ __ __ .

This happened in __ __ __ __ __ .

A century is 100 __ __ __ __ __ .

Write the letters from the colored boxes in the matching boxes below to complete the sentence.

Owen is one  hippo!

# Bird Riddles

Draw a line from each bird riddle on this page to the correct bird on the next page.

My tail is so beautiful! I can fly, but I would rather walk and strut. What am I?

I have feathers and a beak, and I lay eggs like other birds. But I do not fly through the air. I fly through the water! What am I?

I am a beautiful bird, too! I have a sharp beak. If you are patient, you might be able to teach me to say, "Polly want a cracker." What am I?

I am tall. I have a long neck. My feathers are pink from the pink shrimp I like to eat. What am I?

I am a small bird. The feathers on my chest are red. You see me in the spring. What am I?

I have a red comb on top of my head. In the early morning you might hear me call, "cock-a-doodle-do!" What am I?

# From Egg to Frog

Read about the **life cycle** of the frog.

A frog lays its eggs in the water.

Day 6 to day 21: The frog eggs hatch in the water and a tadpole comes out. It uses its tail to swim and breathes through its gills.

Between 12 and 16 weeks: The adult frog is fully grown. Now it uses its lungs to breathe. It lives on land.

Week 12: The tadpole is a young frog, or froglet. It has a short stub of a tail.

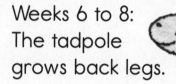

Weeks 6 to 8: The tadpole grows back legs.

Week 9: The tadpole now has front and back legs. It looks like a tiny frog with a long tail. Its lungs begin to grow.

Life cycle

**Science**

Match the words on the frog with the
definitions on the lily pads.

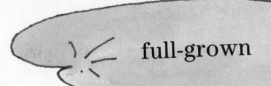

froglet

tadpole

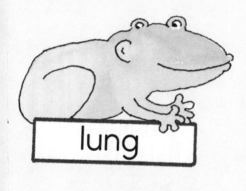

lung

tail

adult

full-grown

body part that helps a
frog breathe

what hatches from
a frog egg

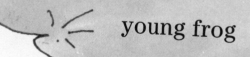
young frog

body part that helps a
tadpole swim

Life cycle

**Science**

# The Camel's a Mammal

Read about **mammals.**

**All Mammals:**

✓ breathe air through lungs.

✓ are born alive. They do not hatch.

✓ drink milk their mothers make.

✓ have hair. Some are born with hair and lose it as they grow up.

Circle all the mammals.

Most mammals live on land, but some mammals live in the sea.

Sea mammals have lungs. They swim up to the surface to breathe air.

Sea creatures that are not mammals do not need to breathe air.

Circle the sea creatures that are mammals.

# Hey, Shelly!

Read about the snail and the turtle.

## Snail

The snail is not a mammal or a reptile. It is a mollusk. The snail's body is soft, but it's protected by a hard shell. How does the snail move? Very slowly! That's because it has just one foot. This soft, flat foot makes a slimy liquid that helps it crawl. A snail has two pairs of tentacles. It sees with eyespots on its long tentacles. The short tentacles help the snail smell and touch.

## Painted Turtle

The painted turtle lives in a large group. It lives in slow-moving rivers with soft, muddy bottoms. The turtle is a reptile with a shell. Its hard shell is called a carapace.

When it's cold outside, the turtle hibernates under the mud. A turtle is slow on land, but its webbed feet help it swim. When danger is near, the turtle pulls its head, legs, and tail inside the shell to protect itself.

Animals with shells

**Science**

Write a fact about how snails and turtles are the same in the green space.

Write a fact about how snails are different in the blue space.

Write a fact about how turtles are different in the yellow space.

Snail

Both

Turtle

Animals with shells

**Science**

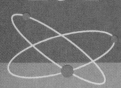

# My Favorite Animal

Complete the sentences.

My favorite animal is _____.

I like it because _____

_____.

Facts I know about it:

1. _____

_____.

2. _____

_____.

3. _____

_____.

Now draw a picture of your favorite animal.

# Answer Key

(For pages not included in this section,
answers will vary.)

## Beginning Letters

Say the word for each picture.
What **beginning sound** do you hear?
Write the letter.

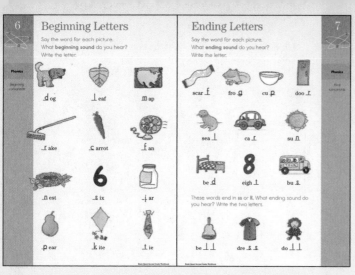

d og     l eaf    m ap

r ake    c arrot    f an

n est    s ix    j ar

p ear    k ite    t ie

## Ending Letters

Say the word for each picture.
What **ending sound** do you hear?
Write the letter.

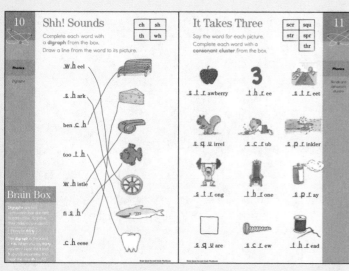

scar f    fro g    cu p    doo r

sea l    ca r    su n

be d    eigh t    bu s

These words end in **ss** or **ll**. What ending sound do
you hear? Write the two letters.

be ll    dre ss    do ll

---

## 8

## It Takes Two

Say the word for each picture.
What **beginning sound** do
you hear?

Find the correct **blend**
in the box. Write it on the line.

| bl | br | cl | cr |
|----|----|----|----|
| dr | fl | fr | gl |
| gr | pl | pr | sc |
| sl | sk | sm | sp |
| st | sw | tr | |

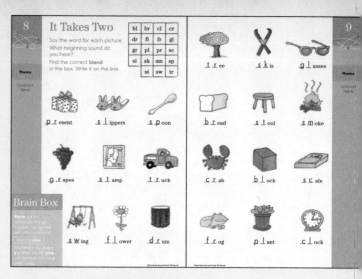

p r esent    s l ippers    s p oon

g r apes    st amp    tr uck

s w ing    f l ower    dr um

### Brain Box

**Blends** are two
consonants that go
together. You can hear
both sounds in a blend.

Example: **plane**.

You can hear the /p/ and
/l/ when you say **plane**.
The letters /p/ and /l/ help
you blend the two sounds.

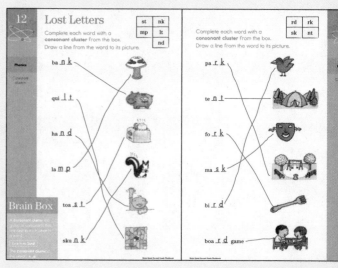

tr ee    sk is    gl asses

br ead    st ool    sm oke

cr ab    bl ock    sc ale

fr og    pl ant    cl ock

---

## Shh! Sounds

| ch | sh |
|----|----|
| th | wh |

Complete each word with a
**digraph** from the box.
Draw a line from the word to its picture.

w h eel

s h ark

ben c h

too t h

w h istle

fi s h

c h eese

### Brain Box

Digraphs are two
consonants that are next
to each other. Together,
they make a new sound.
Example: **thing**.

The **digraph** in the word
**this**, when you say /th/,
you don't hear the /t/ and
/h/ sounds separately. You
hear the new sound.

## 11

## It Takes Three

| scr | squ |
|-----|-----|
| str | spr |
| thr | |

Say the word for each picture.
Complete each word with a
**consonant cluster** from the box.

str awberry    thr ee    str eet

squ irrel    scr ub    spr inkler

str ong    thr one    spr ay

squ are    scr ew    thr ead

---

## Lost Letters

| st | nk |
|----|----|
| mp | lt |
| nd | |

Complete each word with a
**consonant cluster** from the box.
Draw a line from the word to its picture.

ba nk

qui lt

ha nd

la mp

toa st

sku nk

### Brain Box

A consonant cluster has
a group of consonants that
are next to each other in
a word.

Example: **band**.

The consonant cluster in
this word is /nd/.

| rd | rk |
|----|----|
| sk | nt |

Complete each word with a
**consonant cluster** from the box.
Draw a line from the word to its picture.

pa rk

te nt

fo rk

ma sk

bi rd

boa rd game

---

## 14

## Kite and Circle

Look at the **c** words in the Word Box.
If the word has a **hard c** sound, like **kite**,
write the word next to the kite.
If the word has a **soft c** sound, like **circle**,
write the word next to the circle.

come

count

care

card

| come | cent |
|------|------|
| count | care |
| cellar | card |
| city | cereal |

cellar

city

cent

cereal

### Brain Box

The letter **c** has two
sounds: a hard c sound
as in **cat** and a soft c
sound as in **cent**.

## 15

## Goose and Jacket

Look at the **g** words in the Word Box.
If the word has a **hard g** sound, like **goose**,
write the word next to the goose.
If the word has a **soft g** sound, like **jacket**,
write the word next to the jacket.

giraffe

genius

gem

giant

| game | goat |
|------|------|
| giraffe | gem |
| give | giant |
| genius | grow |

game

give

goat

grow

### Brain Box

The letter **g** has two
sounds: a hard g sound
as in **goose** and a soft g
sound as in **giant**.

---

## 16

## Picture Cards

Complete each word with a **short vowel**.

**short a words**

c a t    m a n

h a m    a nt

m a d    b a t

**short e words**

d e sk    b e ll

sl e d    b e d

h e n    p e n

**short i words**

f i sh    w i g

f i ll    p i g

l i d    h i d

**short o words**

d o ll    h o p

r o ck    f o x

n o t    p o t

**short u words**

pl u m    m u d

c u p    b u s

s u n    f u n

---

## Short Vowel Sort

Read the words in the Word Boxes.
Write each word next to the picture that has the
same **short vowel** sound.

| hat | map | big | got | dad |
|-----|-----|-----|-----|-----|
| box | red | hug | miss | let |

**short a words**

hat

hat

map

dad

ran

red

let

pet

ten

**short e words**

chest

| must | pet | mom | up | ran |
|------|-----|-----|----|-----|
| ten | top | rush | him | fix |

miss

him

fix

big

**short i words**

milk

got

box

mom

tap

**short o words**

socks

hug

must

up

rush

**short u words**

umbrella

---

## Ray Takes the Train

Write **ai** or **ay** to complete the **long a** words.

Ray wakes up to the sound of a bluej ay .

He eats cereal on his breakfast tr ay .

He takes the tr ai n
to the beach.

At the beach, Ray puts shells in his p ai l.

Ray loves to pl ay in the water.

He watches a beautiful s ai lboat
float by.

"Wow!" he says. "What a
great d ay !"

### Brain Box

These letter combinations
both make a long a sound.
/ai/ in toast and /ay/ in ray.

## What Do You See?

Write **e**, **ea**, **ee**, or **ey** to complete the **long e** words.

My dad is driving us to the b ea ch.

There are thr ee of us in the car.

On the way w e pass a tr ee .

There are lots of b ee s in the tr ee .

They are making hon ey .

Luckily, the bees don't sting m e !

Finally we reach the s ea !

### Brain Box

These letter combinations
can make a long e sound:
/e/ as in **we**, /ea/ as in
**flea**, /ee/ as in **tree**, and
/ey/ as in **honey**.

Sometimes a letter makes a
long e sound all by itself, as
in the word **me**.

## 22

## I Love Riddles!

Write **i**, **ie**, **igh**, or **y** to complete the long I words.

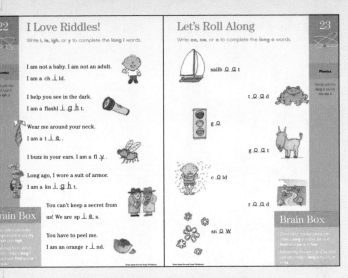

I am not a baby. I am not an adult.
I am a ch **i** ld.

I help you see in the dark.
I am a flashl **igh** t.

Wear me around your neck.
I am a t **ie**.

I buzz in your ears. I am a fl **y**.

Long ago, I wore a suit of armor.
I am a kn **igh** t.

You can't keep a secret from us! We are sp **ie** s.

You have to peel me.
I am an orange r **i** nd.

**Brain Box**

## Let's Roll Along

## 23

Write **oa**, **ow**, or **o** to complete the long **o** words.

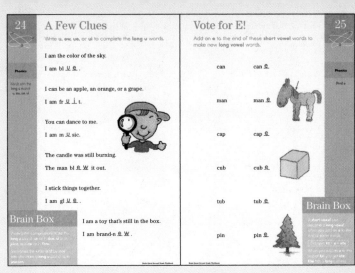

sailb **oa** t

t **oa** d

g **o**

g **oa** t

c **o** ld

r **oa** d

sn **ow**

**Brain Box**

---

## A Few Clues

Write **u**, **ew**, **ue**, or **ui** to complete the long **u** words.

I am the color of the sky.
I am bl **ue**.

I can be an apple, an orange, or a grape.
I am fr **ui** t.

You can dance to me.
I am m **u** sic.

The candle was still burning.
The man bl **ew** it out.

I stick things together.
I am gl **ue**.

I am a toy that's still in the box.
I am brand-n **ew**.

**Brain Box**

## Vote for E!

## 25

Add an **e** to the end of these **short vowel** words to make new **long vowel** words.

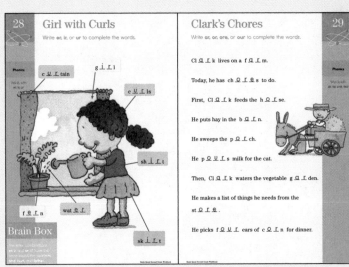

can — can **e**

man — man **e**

cap — cap **e**

cub — cub **e**

tub — tub **e**

pin — pin **e**

**Brain Box**

---

## Mix-Ups

Unscramble each word.
Write the correct word on the line.

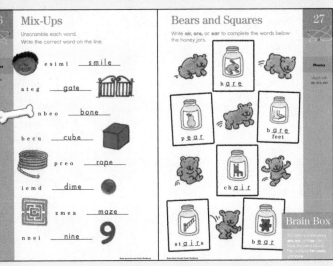

esiml — **smile**

ateg — **gate**

nbeo — **bone**

becu — **cube**

preo — **rope**

iemd — **dime**

zmea — **maze**

nnei — **nine**

## Bears and Squares

Write **air**, **are**, or **ear** to complete the words below the honey jars.

h **are**

p **ear**

b **are** feet

ch **air**

st **air** s

b **ear**

**Brain Box**

---

## Girl with Curls

Write **er**, **ir**, or **ur** to complete the words.

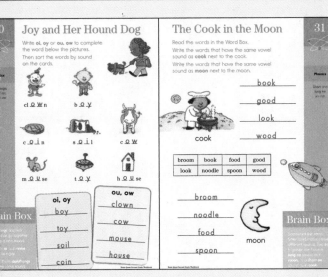

c **ur** tain

g **ir** l

c **ur** ls

sh **ir** t

f **er** n

wat **er**

sk **ir** t

**Brain Box**

## Clark's Chores

## 29

Write **ar**, **or**, **ore**, or **our** to complete the words.

Cl **ar** k lives on a f **ar** m.

Today, he has ch **or** es to do.

First, Cl **ar** k feeds the h **or** se.

He puts hay in the b **ar** n.

He sweeps the p **or** ch.

He p **our** s milk for the cat.

Then, Cl **ar** k waters the vegetable g **ar** den.

He makes a list of things he needs from the st **ore**.

He picks f **our** ears of c **or** n for dinner.

---

## Joy and Her Hound Dog

Write **oi**, **oy** or **ou**, **ow** to complete the word below the pictures.
Then sort the words by sound on the cards.

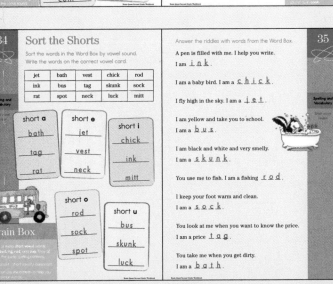

cl **ow** n

b **oy**

c **oi** n

s **oi** l

c **ow**

m **ou** se

t **oy**

h **ou** se

| oi, oy | ou, ow |
|--------|--------|
| boy | clown |
| toy | cow |
| soil | mouse |
| coin | house |

**Brain Box**

## The Cook in the Moon

Read the words in the Word Box.
Write the words that have the same vowel sound as **cook** next to the cook.
Write the words that have the same vowel sound as **moon** next to the moon.

book
good
look
wood

cook

| broom | book | food | good |
|-------|------|------|------|
| look | noodle | spoon | wood |

broom
noodle
food
spoon

moon

**Brain Box**

---

## Rhyme Time!

Write **al**, **all**, **aw**, or **o** to complete each rhyme.

b **all** on the w **all**

w **al** k and t **al** k

m **o** th in the br **o** th

str **aw** on a sees **aw**

l **o** ng s **o** ng

cr **aw** l and b **aw** l

---

## Sort the Shorts

Sort the words in the Word Box by vowel sound.
Write the words on the correct vowel card.

| jet | bath | vest | chick | rod |
|-----|------|------|-------|-----|
| ink | bus | tag | skunk | sock |
| rat | spot | neck | luck | mitt |

**short a**
bath
tag
rat

**short e**
jet
vest
neck

**short i**
chick
ink
mitt

**short o**
rod
sock
spot

**short u**
bus
skunk
luck

**Brain Box**

Answer the riddles with words from the Word Box.

A pen is filled with me. I help you write.
I am **ink**.

I am a baby bird. I am a **chick**.

I fly high in the sky. I am a **jet**.

I am yellow and take you to school.
I am a **bus**.

I am black and white and very smelly.
I am a **skunk**.

You use me to fish. I am a fishing **rod**.

I keep your foot warm and clean.
I am a **sock**.

You look at me when you want to know the price.
I am a price **tag**.

You take me when you get dirty.
I am a **bath**.

---

## Crossword Craze

Complete the long vowel words with a **vowel** and a **final e**.
Write the words in the puzzle.

**Across**

2. She a **t e** the apple.
4. We have a flat t **i** r **e**.
5. A tree with needles: p **i** n **e**.
6. Our whole family gets together on New Year's **e** v **e**.
8. Four plus five equals n **i** n **e**.
9. A raisin is a dried gr **a** p **e**.

**Down**

1. A 3-D map of the world is a gl **o** b **e**.
3. Those are hers, th **e** s **e** are mine.
4. Another word for "melody": t **u** n **e**.
7. Tomatoes grow on a v **i** n **e**.
9. They g **a** v **e** the money they collected to charity.
10. Every Sunday I talk to my grandma on the ph **o** n **e**.

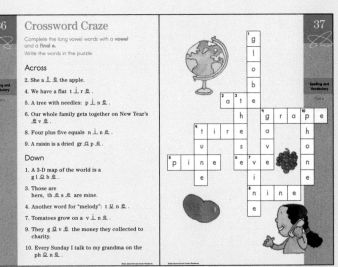

## Long a Words

Complete each sentence with a **long a** word from the Word Box.

Artists like to draw and __paint__ .

The bird is in the __cage__ .

My favorite thing to eat is __cake__ .

I asked the postman for the __mail__ .

We rehearsed our parts for the __play__ .

He fell down, but he is __okay__ .

Word Box: okay, cake, paint, cage, play, mail

Now sort the **long a** words on the cards below.

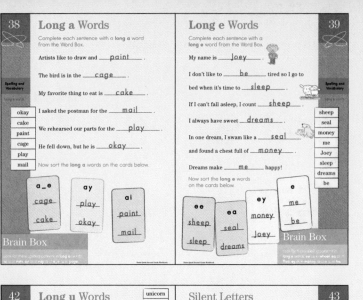

| a_e | ay | ai |
|---|---|---|
| cage | play | paint |
| cake | okay | mail |

### Brain Box

## Long e Words

Complete each sentence with a **long e** word from the Word Box.

My name is __Joey__ .

I don't like to __be__ tired so I go to bed when it's time to __sleep__ .

If I can't fall asleep, I count __sheep__ .

I always have sweet __dreams__ .

In one dream, I swam like a __seal__ and found a chest full of __money__ .

Dreams make __me__ happy!

Word Box: sheep, seal, money, me, Joey, sleep, dreams, be

Now sort the **long e** words on the cards below.

| ee | ea | ey | e |
|---|---|---|---|
| sheep | seal | money | me |
| sleep | dreams | Joey | be |

### Brain Box

---

## Long i Words

Word Box: fries, white, right, blind, lie, bite, night, dry

Complete each sentence with a **long i** word from the Word Box.

I love eating french __fries__ .

My dog does not __bite__ .

The opposite of day is __night__ .

Someone who can't see is __blind__ .

The opposite of wrong is __right__ .

A zebra is black and __white__ .

I tell the truth. I don't __lie__ .

The opposite of wet is __dry__ .

Now sort the **long i** words on the cards below.

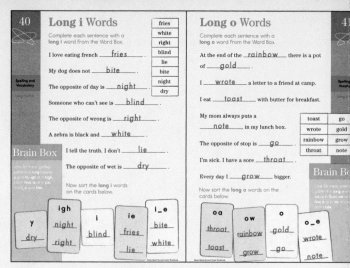

| y | igh | i | ie | i_e |
|---|---|---|---|---|
| dry | night | blind | fries | bite |
| | right | | lie | white |

### Brain Box

## Long o Words

Complete each sentence with a **long o** word from the Word Box.

At the end of the __rainbow__ there is a pot of __gold__ .

I __wrote__ a letter to a friend at camp.

I eat __toast__ with butter for breakfast.

My mom always puts a __note__ in my lunch box.

The opposite of stop is __go__ .

I'm sick. I have a sore __throat__ .

Every day I __grow__ bigger.

Word Box: toast, wrote, rainbow, throat, go, gold, grow, note

Now sort the **long o** words on the cards below.

| oa | ow | o | o_e |
|---|---|---|---|
| throat | rainbow | gold | wrote |
| toast | grow | go | note |

### Brain Box

---

## 41

## Long u Words

Word Box: unicorn, juice, utensils, clue, huge, flew, fruit, cute

Complete each sentence with a **long u** word from the Word Box.

A __unicorn__ has a horn on its head.

I drink orange __juice__ .

A detective follows a __clue__ .

Puppies and kittens are so __cute__ !

The opposite of tiny is __huge__ .

A knife and a fork are eating __utensils__ .

The airplane __flew__ in the sky.

Apples are my favorite __fruit__ .

### Brain Box

Now sort the **long u** words on the cards below.

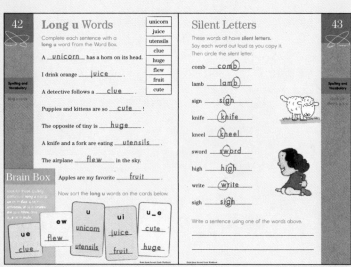

| u | ui | u_e |
|---|---|---|
| unicorn | juice | cute |
| utensils | fruit | huge |

| ew | ue |
|---|---|
| flew | clue |

## Silent Letters

These words all have **silent letters**. Say each word out loud as you copy it. Then circle the silent letter.

comb __com(b)__

lamb __lam(b)__

sign __sig(n)__

knife __(k)nife__

kneel __(k)neel__

sword __s(w)ord__

high __hig(h)__

write __(w)rite__

sigh __sig(h)__

Write a sentence using one of the words above.

_____

---

## Compound It!

Use a word from the Word Box to make a **compound word**. Use the pictures as clues.

pan + __cake__ = pancake

air + __plane__ = airplane

bath + __robe__ = bathrobe

straw + __berry__ = strawberry

key + __hole__ = keyhole

note + __book__ = notebook

flower + __pot__ = flowerpot

gold + __fish__ = goldfish

Word Box: plane, berry, book, fish, pot, hole, robe, cake

### Brain Box

Draw a line from each word in column A to a word in column B to make a common **compound word**. Then write the compound word in column C.

| A | B | C |
|---|---|---|
| back | cage | backbone |
| camp | bone | campfire |
| bag | pole | bagpipes |
| book | work | bookcase |
| grape | flakes | grapevine |
| sky | line | skyline |
| home | pipes | homework |
| bean | fire | beanpole |
| bird | case | birdcage |
| snow | vine | snowflakes |

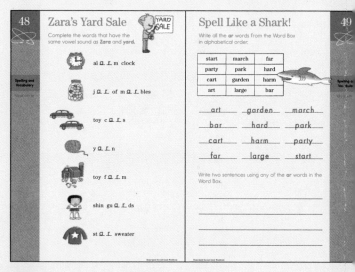

---

## 46

## The Why of Y

The words in the Word Box all end in **y**, but they are not all pronounced the same way. Sort the words by vowel sound. Write the **y** words with the same sound as **bunny** on the bunny card. Write the **y** words with the same sound as **spy** on the spy card.

Word Box: baby, cry, happy, story, fly, mommy, merry, lullaby, my, sky

| bunny | spy |
|---|---|
| baby | cry |
| happy | fly |
| story | lullaby |
| mommy | my |
| merry | sky |

Use words from the Word Box to complete the sentence.

A __mommy__ sings a __lullaby__ to her __baby__ .

## A Silly Story

Read the story. Circle all the words that end in **y**. Then sort the words on the cards below.

There once was a (crazy) (canary). He lived in the (city). In (January), the (tiny) bird decided to (fly) to the (country) to visit his (family). He packed his bag with a (supply) of food, a (library) book, and his favorite (fuzzy) pajamas. Then he flew into the (sky). After months of traveling, he (finally) arrived in (July). Everyone was so (happy).

"Now it's time to go home," chirped the (pretty) bird.

"But (why)?" said his father.

"Because I am (shy)," was his (reply).

| y words with long e sound | y words with long i sound |
|---|---|
| crazy | fly |
| canary | supply |
| city | sky |
| January | July |
| tiny | why |
| country | shy |
| family | reply |
| library | |
| fuzzy | |
| finally | |
| happy | |
| pretty | |

---

## Zara's Yard Sale

Complete the words that have the same vowel sound as **Zara** and **yard**.

al __a r__ m clock

j __a r__ of m __a r__ bles

toy c __a r__ s

y __a r__ n

toy f __a r__ m

shin gu __a r__ ds

st __a r__ sweater

## Spell Like a Shark!

Write all the **ar** words from the Word Box in alphabetical order.

| start | march | far |
|---|---|---|
| party | park | hard |
| cart | garden | harm |
| art | large | bar |

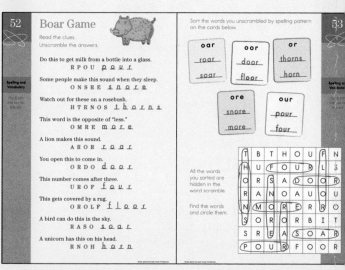

__art__ __garden__ __march__

__bar__ __hard__ __park__

__cart__ __harm__ __party__

__far__ __large__ __start__

Write two sentences using any of the **ar** words in the Word Box.

_____

_____

---

## All About Fern

Circle all the words that have the same vowel sound as **Fern**.

My name is (Fern), and I am the (third) tallest (girl) in my class. I am also the only (person) in my class who has (curly) hair. Can you believe that?

This is my favorite book. I got it for my (birthday). I am (learning) all about Florence Nightingale, the famous (nurse). When I grow up, I want to be a (nurse), too.

Say each word you circled. Listen to the vowel sound. Sort the words by spelling pattern on the ear, er, ir, ur cards below.

| ear | ir | ur |
|---|---|---|
| learning | third | curly |
| | girl | nurse |

| er |
|---|
| Fern |
| person |

## Spell Like a Bird

Say each word in the Word Box. Sort the words by spelling pattern on the cards below.

| pearl | lavender | letter | glitter |
|---|---|---|---|
| lantern | search | earth | urgent |
| burn | first | purpose | early |
| bird | hurt | chirp | dirty |
| curb | shirt | perfect | earn |

| ir | ur | er | ear |
|---|---|---|---|
| first | urgent | lavender | search |
| bird | burn | letter | earth |
| chirp | purpose | glitter | pearl |
| dirty | hurt | lantern | earn |
| shirt | curb | perfect | early |

---

## Boar Game

Read the clues. Unscramble the answers.

Do this to get milk from a bottle into a glass.
R P O U __pour__

Some people make this sound when they sleep.
O N S R E __snore__

Watch out for these on a rosebush.
H T R N O S __thorns__

This word is the opposite of "less."
O M R E __more__

A lion makes this sound.
A R O R __roar__

You open this to come in.
O R D O __door__

This number comes after four.
U R O F __four__

This gets covered by a rug.
O R O L F __floor__

A bird can do this in the sky.
R A S O __soar__

A unicorn has this on his head.
R N O H __horn__

Sort the words you unscrambled by spelling pattern on the cards below.

| oar | oor | or |
|---|---|---|
| roar | door | thorns |
| soar | floor | horn |

| ore | our |
|---|---|
| snore | pour |
| more | four |

All the words you sorted are hidden in the word scramble. Find the words and circle them.

```
T B T H O U F N
H U (F O U R) S S
O R S A D O O R
R A N O A U O U
N (M O R E) R R O
S O R O R B I T
S R E A S O A R
(P O U R) F O O R
```

## A Cow in the House!

Complete the clues with words that have the same spelling pattern as **how** and **mouth**.
Write the words in the puzzle.

### Across

1. Milk comes from c O W S .
3. A h O U S E is a building where you live.
5. Is your hair the color br O W N ?
7. What goes up must come d O W N .
9. A circus cl O W N makes people laugh.
11. I use a t O W E L to get dry.

### Down

2. A tiny animal that likes cheese is a m O U S E .
4. If you lose something, go to the lost and f O U N D .
6. The opposite of "in" is O U T .
8. The opposite of "later" is n O W .
10. To yell something is to sh O U T .
12. A king wears a cr O W N on his head.
13. The opposite of "quiet" is l O U D .
14. A type of bird that goes hoot is an o W L .

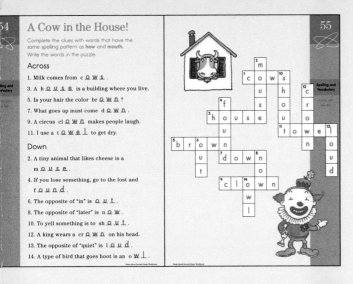

Spelling and Vocabulary

---

## Roy Points

Sort the words by spelling pattern on the cards below.

| coin | oyster | boil | enjoy |
|------|--------|------|-------|
| boy | noise | royal | choice |
| toy | join | point | annoy |
| voice | oil | loyal | destroy |

**oi**
coin          oil
voice         boil
noise         point
join          choice

**oy**
boy           enjoy
toy           loyal
oyster        annoy
royal         destroy

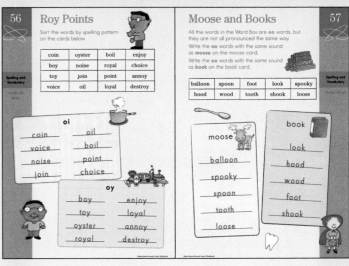

Spelling and Vocabulary

---

## Moose and Books

All the words in the Word Box are **oo** words, but they are not all pronounced the same way.
Write the **oo** words with the same sound as **moose** on the moose card.
Write the **oo** words with the same sound as **book** on the book card.

| balloon | spoon | foot | look | spooky |
|---------|-------|------|------|--------|
| hood | wood | tooth | shook | loose |

**moose**
balloon
spooky
spoon
tooth
loose

**book**
look
hood
wood
foot
shook

Spelling and Vocabulary

---

## Opposites!

Read each sentence.
Color the **antonym** of the underlined word in the sentence.

A great dane is a large dog!
small | giant | big

The balloon flew up in the air.
high | down | left

She went to the front of the line.
top | start | back

It is so hot today!
warm | cold | rainy

Draw a line from each word to its **antonym**.

terrible        dry
before        thrilled
disappointed    after
soaked        fabulous

Brain Box

---

## So Many Snowflakes!

Draw a line from each snowflake to its **synonym**.

correct — right
little — small
a lot — much
great — terrific
gone — went
also — too
speak — say

Fill in the blanks with **synonyms** from the Word Box.

lost _missing_
shine _sparkle_
difficult _challenging_
damp _moist_

| challenging |
| sparkle |
| moist |
| missing |

Spelling and Vocabulary

Brain Box

---

## Write It Right

Circle the correct **homophone** in each sentence.

It is half past the (our / hour).

There is a (pair) / pear tree in the yard.

She broke her (right) / write leg.

The clouds are hiding the son / (sun).

On the lines below, write two sentences for two of the words you did not circle.

_____
_____
_____

Brain Box

---

## Same Sounds

Circle the correct **homophone** in each sentence.

I am going to ballet class, (too) / two.

Look at that fish's I / (eye).

All the boats are on sale / (sail).

The movie is playing for two weaks / (weeks) only.

On the lines below, write two sentences for two of the words you did not circle.

_____
_____
_____

Spelling and Vocabulary

---

## More than One

Write the **plural** for each word by adding **s** or **es**.

apple _apples_       ax _axes_
glass _glasses_       box _boxes_
cat _cats_       sandwich _sandwiches_
fox _foxes_       pen _pens_
brush _brushes_       crutch _crutches_
watch _watches_       bus _buses_

Brain Box

---

## Plural Math

Subtract and add letters to spell the **irregular plural** of each word.

foot
– oo
+ ee
= f e e t

woman
– a
+ e
= w o m e n

die
+ c
= d i c e

child
+ ren
= c h i l d r e n

tooth
– oo
+ ee
= t e e t h

mouse
– ous
+ ic
= m i c e

Brain Box

---

## Color Search

Circle all the **color words** in the puzzle.

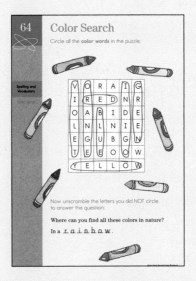

Now unscramble the letters you did NOT circle to answer this question:

Where can you find all these colors in nature?

In a r a i n b o w .

Spelling and Vocabulary

---

## Tell Me About It!

Read each group of words.
Underline the **statements**.

<u>I like to go to the ice-cream store.</u>

The pictures on the window.

My mother, my sister, and I.

<u>We eat our favorite flavors.</u>

The chocolate ice cream.

<u>I sit on the bench.</u>

<u>My mom likes vanilla.</u>

The books resting by our feet.

<u>I have red shoes.</u>

Brain Box

Language Arts

---

Write each statement correctly.

the swimming class begins at noon
_The swimming class begins at noon._

i can dive off the high board.
_I can dive off the high board_

Sara does a backflip
_Sara does a backflip._

the little kids wear water wings
_The little kids wear water wings._

our lifeguard's name is Rena
_Our lifeguard's name is Rena._

---

## Say What?

Rewrite each sentence.
If the sentence asks a **question**, add a question mark.
If the sentence is a **statement**, add a period.

is it raining hard
_Is it raining hard?_

sam likes his green boots
_Sam likes his green boots._

can we jump in the puddles
_Can we jump in the puddles?_

will you play with me after school
_Will you play with me after school?_

i hope it stops raining
_I hope it stops raining._

what did the weather forecast say
_What did the weather forecast say?_

do you see a rainbow
_Do you see a rainbow?_

Brain Box

Language Arts

---

## The Race Begins!

Rewrite each sentence as an **exclamation**.

look how fast I can run
_Look how fast I can run!_

tie your shoelaces
_Tie your shoelaces!_

we love racing
_We love racing!_

on your mark, get set, go
_On your mark, get set, go!_

hurry to the finish line
_Hurry to the finish line!_

Oh, no! Jamal is still reading when he should be going to sleep.
Write two **commands** that his father might say to him.

Language Arts

Brain Box

---

## 70

## A Picture Tells a Story

Write each sentence correctly.
Then circle the type of sentence it is.

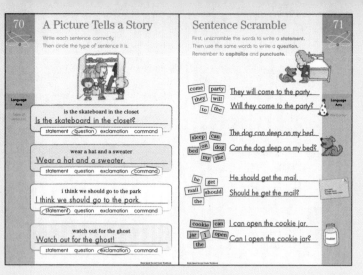

is the skateboard in the closet
**Is the skateboard in the closet?**
statement (question) exclamation command

wear a hat and a sweater
**Wear a hat and a sweater.**
statement question exclamation (command)

i think we should go to the park
**I think we should go to the park.**
(statement) question exclamation command

watch out for the ghost
**Watch out for the ghost!**
statement question (exclamation) command

## Sentence Scramble

First, unscramble the words to write a **statement**.
Then use the same words to write a **question**.
Remember to **capitalize** and **punctuate**.

come party they will to the
**They will come to the party.**
**Will they come to the party?**

sleep can bed on dog my
**The dog can sleep on my bed.**
**Can the dog sleep on my bed?**

he get mail should the
**He should get the mail.**
**Should he get the mail?**

cookie can jar I open the
**I can open the cookie jar.**
**Can I open the cookie jar?**

## 72

## People in Town

Underline the **common nouns** in each sentence.

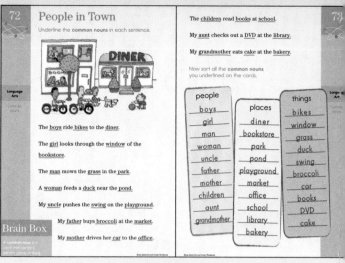

The boys ride bikes to the diner.

The girl looks through the window of the bookstore.

The man mows the grass in the park.

A woman feeds a duck near the pond.

My uncle pushes the swing on the playground.

My father buys broccoli at the market.

My mother drives her car to the office.

**Brain Box**

## 73

The children read books at school.

My aunt checks out a DVD at the library.

My grandmother eats cake at the bakery.

Now sort all the **common nouns** you underlined on the cards.

| people | places | things |
|---|---|---|
| boys | diner | bikes |
| girl | bookstore | window |
| man | park | grass |
| woman | pond | duck |
| uncle | playground | swing |
| father | market | broccoli |
| mother | office | car |
| children | school | books |
| aunt | library | DVD |
| grandmother | bakery | cake |

## 74

## And Away We Go!

Underline the **proper nouns** in each sentence.

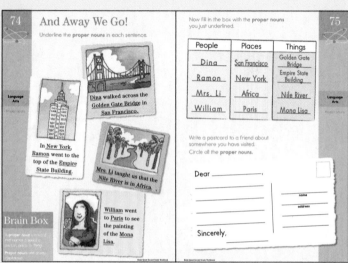

Dina walked across the Golden Gate Bridge in San Francisco.

In New York, Ramon went to the top of the Empire State Building.

Mrs. Li taught us that the Nile River is in Africa.

William went to Paris to see the painting of the Mona Lisa.

**Brain Box**

## 75

Now fill in the box with the **proper nouns** you just underlined.

| People | Places | Things |
|---|---|---|
| Dina | San Francisco | Golden Gate Bridge |
| Ramon | New York | Empire State Building |
| Mrs. Li | Africa | Nile River |
| William | Paris | Mona Lisa |

Write a postcard to a friend about somewhere you have visited.
Circle all the **proper nouns**.

Dear _____

_____
_____
_____

Sincerely,

name
address

## 77

## Fun at the Playground!

The words on the balls are all **pronouns**.
Rewrite each sentence using the pronoun that can take the place of the underlined word(s) in each sentence.

She We They It He

Max and Lila are on the seesaw.
**They are on the seesaw.**

Juan swings through the air.
**He swings through the air.**

Amy zooms down the slide.
**She zooms down the slide.**

All of us are having a good time.
**We are having a good time.**

The playground is busy.
**It is busy.**

**Brain Box**

## 78

## Dog Day

Underline the **subject** of each sentence.
Circle the **noun**.

The (park) is a busy place.

Ollie walks his (dogs) there every afternoon.

The biggest (dog) is named Hamlet.

Ollie's favorite is a (poodle) named Fifi.

The (pets) run and play together.

Some (dogs) bark at the squirrels.

The (squirrels) stay in the trees.

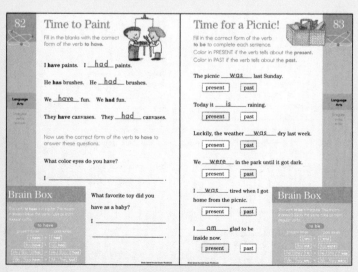

**Brain Box**

## 79

## Batter Up!

Use the words on the baseballs to complete the sentences.

swings holds hits steps picks throws

The batter **picks** up the bat.

She **steps** up to home plate.

The catcher **holds** up her mitt.

The pitcher **throws** the ball.

The batter **swings**.

She **hits** the ball.

**Brain Box**

Write a sentence describing your favorite sport.
Underline the **verb** in your sentence.

_____
_____

## Now and Then

Underline the **verb** in each sentence.

Minx jumps up on the dresser.

Minx moves the book with her paw.

The book falls on the floor.

Jinx picks up the book.

He takes it into the living room.

Jinx licks the cover.

What will Jinx or Minx do next?
Write a sentence with a **present tense verb**.
Underline the **verb** in your sentence.

_____
_____

**Brain Box**

## 81

Minx and Jinx got into trouble yesterday, too!
Change the underlined **verb** to tell about the **past**.

Jinx licks his paw.
Yesterday, Jinx **licked** his paw.

Jinx chews Marc's book.
Yesterday, Jinx **chewed** Marc's book.

Minx claws the cover.
Minx **clawed** the cover.

Marc walks into the room.
Marc **walked** into the room.

He picks up the book.
He **picked** up the book.

Marc scolds Jinx and Minx.
Marc **scolded** Jinx and Minx.

Marc needs a new book.
Marc **needed** a new book.

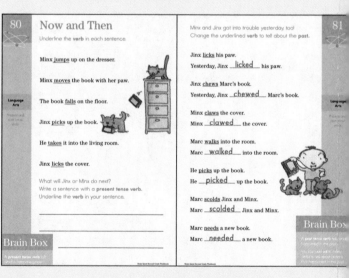

**Brain Box**

## Time to Paint

Fill in the blanks with the correct form of the verb **to have**.

I **have** paints. I **had** paints.

He **has** brushes. He **had** brushes.

We **have** fun. We **had** fun.

They **have** canvases. They **had** canvases.

Now use the correct form of the verb **to have** to answer these questions.

What color eyes do you have?

I _____

What favorite toy did you have as a baby?

I _____

**Brain Box**

## Time for a Picnic!

Fill in the correct form of the verb **to be** to complete each sentence.
Color in PRESENT if the verb tells about the **present**.
Color in PAST if the verb tells about the **past**.

The picnic **was** last Sunday.
present | past

Today it **is** raining.
present | past

Luckily, the weather **was** dry last week.
present | past

We **were** in the park until it got dark.
present | past

I **was** tired when I got home from the picnic.
present | past

I **am** glad to be inside now.
present | past

**Brain Box**

## To Have and To Be

Use a form of **to be** or **to have** to answer each question.

What is the weather like today?

_____

What was the weather like yesterday?

_____

Do you have an umbrella today?

_____

Draw a picture of you and a friend from school in the picture frame.
Then answer the questions below.

I **am** **8** years old.

My best friend **is** _____ years old.

This year, we **are** in the _____ grade.

Last year, we **were** in the _____ grade.

## Who Did What?

Use the drawings to help you match the **subjects** to the **predicates**.
Draw a line from the words in the SUBJECT column to the matching words in the PREDICATE column.

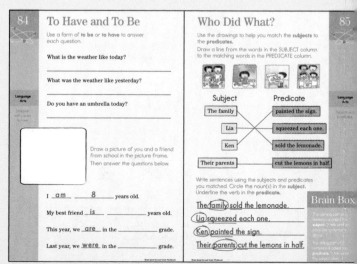

| Subject | Predicate |
|---|---|
| The family | painted the sign. |
| Lia | squeezed each one. |
| Ken | sold the lemonade. |
| Their parents | cut the lemons in half. |

Write sentences using the subjects and predicates you matched. Circle the noun(s) in the **subject**. Underline the verb in the **predicate**.

The (family) sold the lemonade.

(Lia) squeezed each one.

(Ken) painted the sign.

Their (parents) cut the lemons in half.

**Brain Box**

Brain Quest Second Grade Workbook

## 86

## Day at the Carnival

Look at each picture and read the caption.
Circle the **noun**.
Underline the **adjective**.

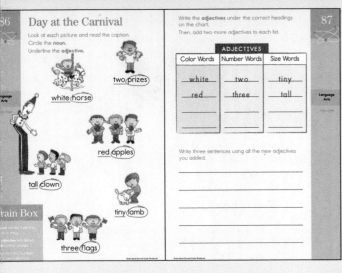

two prizes

white horse

red apples

tall clown

tiny lamb

three flags

**Brain Box**
...

Write the **adjectives** under the correct headings on the chart.
Then, add two more adjectives to each list.

**ADJECTIVES**

| Color Words | Number Words | Size Words |
|---|---|---|
| white | two | tiny |
| red | three | tall |
| | | |
| | | |

Write three sentences using all the new adjectives you added.

_____
_____
_____
_____
_____
_____

*Language Arts*

## 88

## Five Senses

Circle the **noun** in each caption.
Underline the **adjective**.

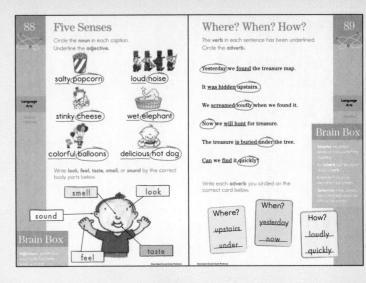

salty popcorn

loud noise

stinky cheese

wet elephant

colorful balloons

delicious hot dog

Write **look, feel, taste, smell,** or **sound** by the correct body parts below.

smell

look

sound

feel

taste

**Brain Box**
Adjectives...

*Language Arts*

## 89

## Where? When? How?

The **verb** in each sentence has been underlined.
Circle the **adverb**.

Yesterday we found the treasure map.

It was hidden upstairs.

We screamed loudly when we found it.

Now we will hunt for treasure.

The treasure is buried under the tree.

Can we find it quickly?

Write each **adverb** you circled on the correct card below.

**Where?**
upstairs
under

**When?**
yesterday
now

**How?**
loudly
quickly

**Brain Box**
Adverbs...

*Language Arts*

## 90

## Bear Bakes

Underline the **verb** in each sentence.
Circle the **adverb**.

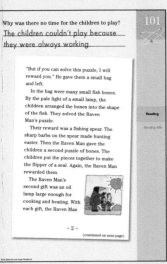

Bear went inside to bake apples.

He washed the apples carefully.

Afterward he put them in the oven.

Later he saw they were done.

He took the tray from the oven slowly.

He will sell the apples outside at the market.

Write each **adverb** you circled on the correct card below.

**Where?**
inside
outside

**When?**
afterward
later

**How?**
carefully
slowly

*Language Arts*

"Bed in Summer" is a poem that rhymes.
Fill in the chart with **rhyming words** that end the lines of the poem. Then add your own rhyming word.

night
candlelight

way
day
play

see
tree

feet
street

you
blue

Now answer the questions.

How does the child in the poem feel?
_____
_____

How do you feel in the summertime?
_____
_____

*Reading*

"Yes!" said Wind. "We will have a contest!"

Sun looked down and saw an old man strolling by. He wore a hat and an overcoat. "Do you see that old man?" Sun asked. "Whichever of us can make him take off his overcoat is the strongest. Wind, I will let you go first." Then Sun hid behind a cloud to watch.

Wind huffed. Wind puffed. Wind began to blow. The trees bowed down even lower. The windows in the farmhouse shook louder. Wind blew strong and cold.

The man said, "Brrr! What a cold, strong wind!" Then he buttoned up his overcoat.

Wind blew stronger. Wind blew colder.

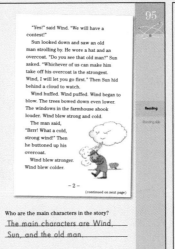

– 2 –

(continued on next page)

Who are the main characters in the story?
The main characters are Wind,
Sun, and the old man.

*Reading*

What do Sun and Wind want to do?
They want to make the old man take
his coat off.

What happened when Wind blew?
The old man buttoned his overcoat.
_____

What happened when Sun shone?
The old man took off his overcoat.
_____

Who won the contest?
Sun won the contest.

What would happen if Rain came along and entered the contest?
_____
_____

How does having a contest solve an argument?
_____
_____

*Reading*

## 101

Why was there no time for the children to play?
The children couldn't play because
they were always working.

"But if you can solve this puzzle, I will reward you." He gave them a small bag and left.

In the bag were many small fish bones. By the pale light of a small lamp, the children arranged the bones into the shape of the fish. They solved the Raven Man's puzzle.

Their reward was a fishing spear. The sharp barbs on the spear made hunting easier. Then the Raven Man gave the children a second puzzle of bones. The children put the pieces together to make the flipper of a seal. Again, the Raven Man rewarded them.

The Raven Man's second gift was an oil lamp large enough for cooking and heating. With each gift, the Raven Man

– 2 –

(continued on next page)

*Reading*

made life a little easier for the children. Then the Raven Man took out a ball. He said, "Now let's play."

Outside in the freezing darkness, the children and the Raven Man played catch. Suddenly the ball caught on the Raven Man's sharp beak. The ball ripped open. Through the tear, the sun escaped and lit the sky. For the first time, the world felt the warmth of sunshine.

And that is how day was created out of night.

THE END

– 3 –

What was inside the ball the children were playing with?
The sun was in the ball.

*Reading*

What two gifts did the Raven Man give the children?
The Raven Man gave the children a
fishing spear and an oil lamp.

How do you think the children feel at the end of the story? Why?
_____
_____

How would this story ending be different if the visitor were a Rabbit Man instead of the Raven Man?
_____
_____

What happened first, next, and last?
Number the pictures to show the order:

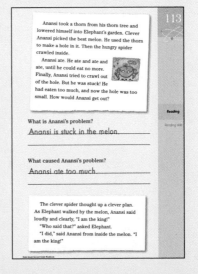

*Reading*

Plot the play you just read.
Tell what happens in the **beginning, middle,** and **end** of the play.

**Beginning** Why won't the old man let the young man rest under the tree?
The old man tells the young man that
he owns the tree and its shade.

**Middle** What does the young man do next?
The young man buys the shade.

**End** How does the story end?
Everyone enjoys the shade of the
tree.

Can you think of a different ending for the story? Write it here.
_____
_____

*Reading*

Draw a line to match each **cause** and **effect**.

**Causes**

Lena learned it was going to rain.

Grace and Justin play soccer on Monday.

Lena, Grace, and Justin are friends.

**Effects**

They put their shin guards in their backpacks.

They talk and joke together.

She took an umbrella to school.

Write three other titles for this story.
Circle the one you like best.
_____
_____
_____

*Reading*

Who is who?
Write the name of the character in the picture on the line.

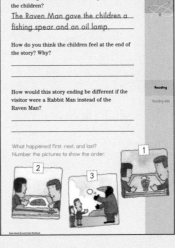
Pecos Bill

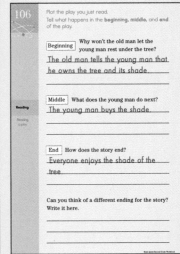
Paul Bunyan

Pecos Bill

Paul Bunyan

*Reading*

Anansi took a thorn from his thorn tree and lowered himself into Elephant's garden. Clever Anansi picked the best melon. He used the thorn to make a hole in it. Then the hungry spider crawled inside.

Anansi ate. He ate and ate and ate, until he could eat no more. Finally, Anansi tried to crawl out of the hole. But he was stuck! He had eaten too much, and now the hole was too small. How would Anansi get out?

What is Anansi's problem?
Anansi is stuck in the melon.

What caused Anansi's problem?
Anansi ate too much.

The clever spider thought up a clever plan.
As Elephant walked by the melon, Anansi said loudly and clearly, "I am the king!"
"Who said that?" asked Elephant.
"I did," said Anansi from inside the melon. "I am the king!"

*Reading*

Brain Quest Second Grade Workbook

## 162 Bundles of Bugs

Look at the **numerals** and words on each jar.
Write the number they equal on the line.

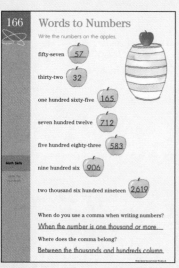

1 ten + 7 ones = 17

3 tens + 8 ones = 38

7 tens + 0 ones = 70

9 tens + 3 ones = 93

Math Skills

### Brain Box

You can use **place value** to figure out how much numerals are equal to. Look at 36:

```
tens  ones
 3     6
```

The 3 is a **ten**, or **3 tens**.
The 6 is a **one**, or **6 ones**.

---

## Hop to It!  163

Circle the correct **numeral**.

Circle the ones.     12③
Circle the tens.     ④5
Circle the hundreds. ⑧36
Circle the tens.     5①7
Circle the hundreds. ③82
Circle the ones.     69⑦

Write the place value for each numeral on the chart.

|     | hundreds | tens | ones |
|-----|----------|------|------|
| 624 | 6 | 2 | 4 |
| 391 | 3 | 9 | 1 |
| 105 | 1 | 0 | 5 |
| 879 | 8 | 7 | 9 |
| 243 | 2 | 4 | 3 |

Math Skills

### Brain Box

If you see three numerals, you know that the number is made up of ones, tens, and ones. Look at 834.

```
hundreds  tens  ones
   8        3     4
```

The 8 is worth 8 **hundreds**. The 3 are **tens** and 2 ten.
The 4 is worth four or **4 ones**.

---

## 164 Lucky Thousands

Write the **place value** for each numeral on the chart.

|       | thousands | hundreds | tens | ones |
|-------|-----------|----------|------|------|
| 1,843 | 1 | 8 | 4 | 3 |
| 2,692 | 2 | 6 | 9 | 2 |
| 7,034 | 7 | 0 | 3 | 4 |
| 4,880 | 4 | 8 | 8 | 0 |
| 9,718 | 9 | 7 | 1 | 8 |

Draw a line to match the words to the number.

8 thousands, 5 hundreds, 3 tens, 5 ones → 9,101
9 thousands, 1 hundred, 0 tens, 1 one → 6,464
6 thousands, 4 hundreds, 4 tens, 6 ones → 6,446
6 thousands, 4 hundreds, 6 tens, 4 ones → 8,535

Math Skills

### Brain Box

If you see four numerals, you know that the number is made up of thousands, hundreds, tens, and ones. Look at 4,627.

```
thousands  hundreds  tens  ones
    4          6        2     7
```

The 4 is worth 4 thousands. The 6 is worth six 6 hundreds.
The 2 is worth two or 2 tens. The 7 is worth seven or 7 ones.

---

## Words to Numbers  166

Draw a line to match the number to the words.

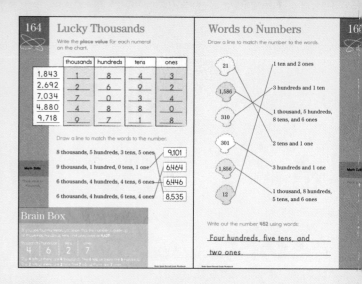

21 — 1 ten and 2 ones
1,586 — 3 hundreds and 1 ten
310 — 1 thousand, 5 hundreds, 8 tens, and 6 ones
301 — 2 tens and 1 one
1,856 — 3 hundreds and 1 one
12 — 1 thousand, 8 hundreds, 5 tens, and 6 ones

Math Skills

Write out the number **452** using words:

Four hundreds, five tens, and
two ones.

---

## 166 Words to Numbers

Write the numbers on the apples.

fifty-seven  57
thirty-two  32
one hundred sixty-five  165
seven hundred twelve  712
five hundred eighty-three  583
nine hundred six  906
two thousand six hundred nineteen  2,619

Math Skills

When do you use a comma when writing numbers?
When the number is one thousand or more

Where does the comma belong?
Between the thousands and hundreds column.

---

## Compare the Candles  169

Write the number of candles beneath each cake.
Then write > or < to show which cake has more.

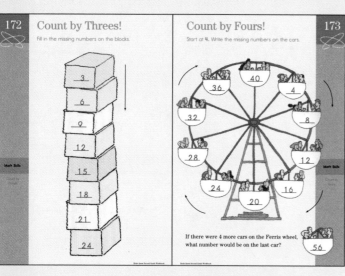

12 < 13

4 < 9

10 > 7

5 < 6

11 > 8

### Brain Box

< means **less than.**

> means **greater than.**

The **less than** sign points to the **lesser** number.
Example: 4 < 8

The **greater than** sign points to the **lesser** number.
Example: 10 > 5

The greater than sign means 10 is greater than 5.

---

## 170 Guess My Age

Write > or < to show who is older.

>

<

<

>

Math Skills

---

## Count by Twos!  171

Fill in the missing numbers on the pearl necklace.

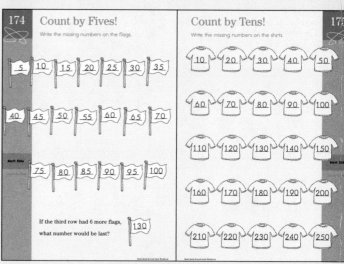

2, 4, 6, 8, 10, 12, 14, 16, 18, 20, 22, 24, 26, 28, 30, 32, 34, 36

---

## 172 Count by Threes!

Fill in the missing numbers on the blocks.

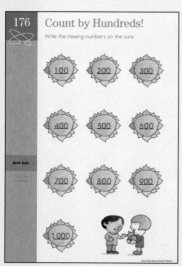

3, 6, 9, 12, 15, 18, 21, 24

Math Skills

---

## Count by Fours!  173

Start at 4. Write the missing numbers on the cars.

4, 8, 12, 16, 20, 24, 28, 32, 36, 40

Math Skills

If there were 4 more cars on the Ferris wheel,
what number would be on the last car?  56

---

## 174 Count by Fives!

Write the missing numbers on the flags.

5, 10, 15, 20, 25, 30, 35
40, 45, 50, 55, 60, 65, 70
75, 80, 85, 90, 95, 100

Math Skills

If the third row had 6 more flags,
what number would be last?  130

---

## Count by Tens!  175

Write the missing numbers on the shirts.

10, 20, 30, 40, 50
60, 70, 80, 90, 100
110, 120, 130, 140, 150
160, 170, 180, 190, 200
210, 220, 230, 240, 250

Math Skills

---

## 176 Count by Hundreds!

Write the missing numbers on the suns.

100, 200, 300
400, 500, 600
700, 800, 900
1,000

Math Skills

---

## 178 Pop That Balloon!

**Add** the numbers in each balloon.
If all the sums equal the number on the basket,
color the balloon any color you like.
If the sums do not equal the number on the basket,
pop the balloon by coloring it black.

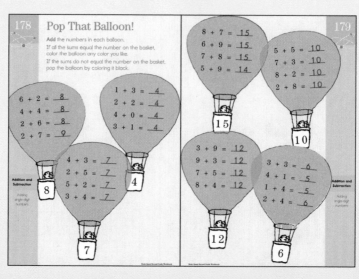

Balloon (basket 8):
6 + 2 = 8
4 + 4 = 8
2 + 6 = 8
2 + 7 = 9

Balloon (basket 4):
1 + 3 = 4
2 + 2 = 4
4 + 0 = 4
3 + 1 = 4

Balloon (basket 7):
4 + 3 = 7
2 + 5 = 7
5 + 2 = 7
3 + 4 = 7

Addition and Subtraction

Adding single-digit numbers.

### 179

Balloon (basket 15):
8 + 7 = 15
6 + 9 = 15
7 + 8 = 15
5 + 9 = 14

Balloon (basket 10):
5 + 5 = 10
7 + 3 = 10
8 + 2 = 10
2 + 8 = 10

Balloon (basket 12):
3 + 9 = 12
9 + 3 = 12
7 + 5 = 12
8 + 4 = 12

Balloon (basket 6):
3 + 3 = 6
4 + 1 = 5
1 + 4 = 5
2 + 4 = 6

Addition and Subtraction

Adding single-digit numbers.

## Go Fish!

Finish the fact families. Write the missing numbers.

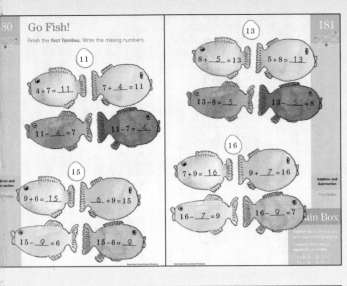

11

$4 + 7 = 11$    $7 + 4 = 11$

$11 - 4 = 7$    $11 - 7 = 4$

15

$9 + 6 = 15$    $- 6 + 9 = 15$

$15 - 9 = 6$    $15 - 6 = 9$

13

$8 + 5 = 13$    $5 + 8 = 13$

$13 - 8 = 5$    $13 - 5 = 8$

16

$7 + 9 = 16$    $9 + 7 = 16$

$16 - 7 = 9$    $16 - 9 = 7$

Addition and Subtraction — Fact families

Brain Box

---

## Tic Tac Total

Add each set of numbers. To win tic-tac-toe, draw a line through the three answers that are the same.

| $11 + 6 = 17$ | $23 + 15 = 38$ | $14 + 4 = 18$ |
|---|---|---|
| $17 + 22 = 39$ | $14 + 3 = 17$ | $21 + 16 = 37$ |
| $20 + 39 = 59$ | $23 + 5 = 28$ | $10 + 7 = 17$ |

| $27 + 22 = 49$ | $14 + 5 = 19$ | $21 + 4 = 25$ |
|---|---|---|
| $10 + 8 = 18$ | $20 + 5 = 25$ | $13 + 6 = 19$ |
| $22 + 3 = 25$ | $10 + 7 = 17$ | $28 + 31 = 59$ |

| $21 + 5 = 26$ | $12 + 18 = 25$ | $23 + 16 = 39$ |
|---|---|---|
| $1 + 6 = 7$ | $10 + 15 = 25$ | $12 + 7 = 19$ |
| $10 + 2 = 12$ | $11 + 1 = 25$ | $18 + 1 = 19$ |

| $13 + 6 = 19$ | $21 + 4 = 25$ | $22 + 12 = 34$ |
|---|---|---|
| $15 + 23 = 38$ | $11 + 0 = 14$ | $12 + 34 = 46$ |
| $20 + 9 = 29$ | $22 + 7 = 29$ | $28 + 1 = 29$ |

Brain Box

Addition and Subtraction — Adding single- and double-digit numbers.

---

## Tic SubTract Toe

Subtract the numbers. To win tic-tac-toe, draw a line through the three answers that are the same.

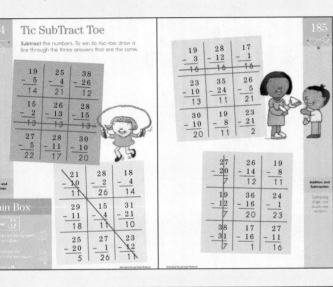

| $19 - 5 = 14$ | $25 - 4 = 21$ | $38 - 26 = 12$ |
|---|---|---|
| $15 - 2 = 13$ | $26 - 13 = 13$ | $28 - 15 = 13$ |
| $27 - 5 = 22$ | $28 - 11 = 17$ | $30 - 10 = 20$ |

| $21 - 10 = 11$ | $28 - 2 = 26$ | $18 - 4 = 14$ |
|---|---|---|
| $29 - 11 = 18$ | $15 - 4 = 11$ | $31 - 21 = 10$ |
| $25 - 20 = 5$ | $27 - 1 = 26$ | $23 - 12 = 11$ |

| $19 - 3 = 16$ | $28 - 12 = 16$ | $17 - 1 = 16$ |
|---|---|---|
| $23 - 10 = 13$ | $35 - 24 = 11$ | $26 - 5 = 21$ |
| $30 - 10 = 20$ | $19 - 8 = 11$ | $23 - 21 = 2$ |

| $27 - 20 = 7$ | $26 - 14 = 12$ | $19 - 8 = 11$ |
|---|---|---|
| $19 - 12 = 7$ | $36 - 16 = 20$ | $24 - 1 = 23$ |
| $38 - 31 = 7$ | $17 - 16 = 1$ | $27 - 11 = 16$ |

Brain Box

Addition and Subtraction — Subtracting single- and double-digit numbers.

---

## Colorful Math

Add or subtract. Then use the key to color the spaces.

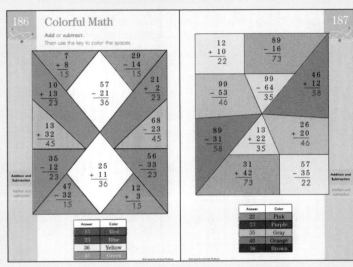

$7 + 8 = 15$    $29 - 14 = 15$

$10 + 13 = 23$    $57 - 21 = 36$    $21 + 2 = 23$

$13 + 32 = 45$    $68 - 23 = 45$

$35 - 12 = 23$    $25 + 11 = 36$    $56 - 33 = 23$

$47 - 32 = 15$    $12 + 3 = 15$

$12 + 10 = 22$    $89 - 16 = 73$

$99 - 53 = 46$    $99 - 64 = 35$    $46 + 12 = 58$

$89 - 31 = 58$    $13 + 22 = 35$    $26 + 20 = 46$

$31 + 42 = 73$    $57 - 35 = 22$

| Answer | Color |
|---|---|
| 22 | Pink |
| 73 | Purple |
| 35 | Gray |
| 46 | Orange |
| 58 | Brown |
| 15 | Red |
| 23 | Blue |
| 36 | Yellow |
| 45 | Green |

Addition and subtraction.

---

## Break the Code

Add or subtract.

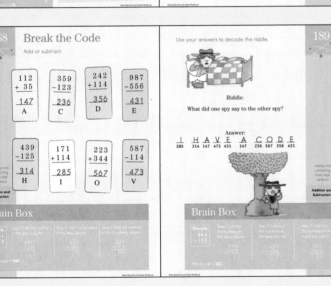

| $112 + 35 = 147$  A | $359 - 123 = 236$  C | $242 + 114 = 356$  D | $987 - 556 = 431$  E |
|---|---|---|---|
| $439 - 125 = 314$  H | $171 + 114 = 285$  I | $223 + 344 = 567$  O | $587 - 114 = 473$  V |

Use your answers to decode the riddle.

Riddle:
What did one spy say to the other spy?

Answer:
I H A V E A   C O D E
285 314 147 473 431   147 236 567 356 431

Brain Box

Addition and Subtraction — Adding and subtracting three-digit numbers.

---

## Math Riddle

Add or subtract.

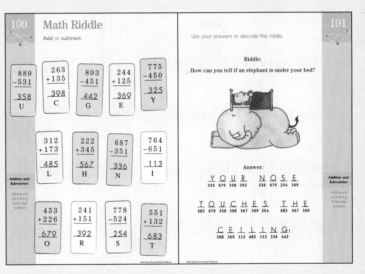

| $889 - 531 = 358$  U | $263 + 135 = 398$  C | $893 - 451 = 442$  G | $244 + 125 = 369$  E | $775 - 450 = 325$  Y |
|---|---|---|---|---|
| $312 + 173 = 485$  L | $222 + 345 = 567$  H | $687 - 351 = 336$  N | $764 - 651 = 113$  I | |
| $453 + 226 = 679$  O | $241 + 151 = 392$  R | $778 - 524 = 254$  S | $551 + 132 = 683$  T | |

Use your answers to decode the riddle.

Riddle:
How can you tell if an elephant is under your bed?

Answer:
Y O U R   N O S E
325 679 254 369   336 679 254 369

T O U C H E S   T H E
683 679 358 398 567 369 254   683 567 369

C E I L I N G!
398 369 113 485 113 336 442

Addition and subtraction — Adding and subtracting three-digit numbers.

---

## Math Pun

Add the numbers using regrouping.

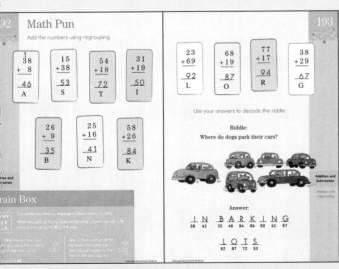

| $38 + 8 = 46$  A | $15 + 38 = 53$  S | $54 + 18 = 72$  T | $31 + 19 = 50$  I |
|---|---|---|---|
| $26 + 9 = 35$  B | $25 + 16 = 41$  N | $58 + 26 = 84$  K | |

| $23 + 69 = 92$  L | $68 + 19 = 87$  O | $77 + 17 = 94$  R | $38 + 29 = 67$  G |
|---|---|---|---|

Use your answers to decode the riddle.

Riddle:
Where do dogs park their cars?

Answer:
I N   B A R K I N G
50 41   35 46 94 50 41 67

L O T S
92 87 72 53

Brain Box

Addition and Subtraction — Addition with regrouping.

---

## Boat Bingo

Subtract using regrouping. Color the cards with the answers that match the card on the right.

58

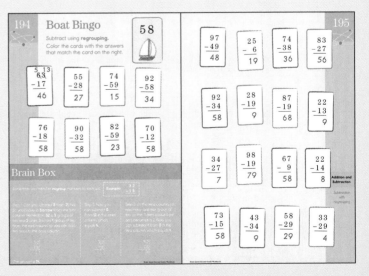

| $63 - 17 = 46$ | $55 - 28 = 27$ | $74 - 59 = 15$ | $92 - 58 = 34$ |
|---|---|---|---|
| $76 - 18 = 58$ | $90 - 32 = 58$ | $82 - 59 = 23$ | $70 - 12 = 58$ |

| $97 - 49 = 48$ | $25 - 6 = 19$ | $74 - 38 = 36$ | $83 - 27 = 56$ |
|---|---|---|---|
| $92 - 34 = 58$ | $28 - 19 = 9$ | $87 - 19 = 68$ | $22 - 13 = 9$ |
| $34 - 27 = 7$ | $98 - 19 = 79$ | $67 - 9 = 58$ | $22 - 14 = 8$ |
| $73 - 15 = 58$ | $43 - 34 = 9$ | $58 - 29 = 29$ | $33 - 29 = 4$ |

Brain Box

Addition and Subtraction — Subtraction with regrouping.

# Hundreds of Gum Balls

Add the numbers using regrouping.

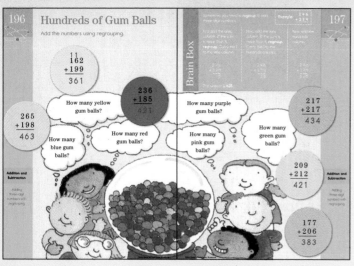

$$\begin{array}{r}11\\162\\+199\\\hline 361\end{array}$$

$$\begin{array}{r}236\\+185\\\hline 421\end{array}$$

$$\begin{array}{r}265\\+198\\\hline 463\end{array}$$

How many yellow gum balls?

How many purple gum balls?

How many red gum balls?

How many blue gum balls?

How many pink gum balls?

How many green gum balls?

$$\begin{array}{r}217\\+217\\\hline 434\end{array}$$

$$\begin{array}{r}209\\+212\\\hline 421\end{array}$$

$$\begin{array}{r}177\\+206\\\hline 383\end{array}$$

Addition and Subtraction

## Brain Box

---

# Aye, Aye, Captain!

Subtract using regrouping.

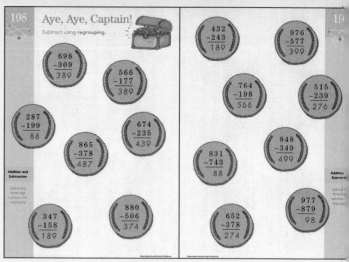

$$\begin{array}{r}698\\-309\\\hline 389\end{array}$$

$$\begin{array}{r}566\\-177\\\hline 389\end{array}$$

$$\begin{array}{r}287\\-199\\\hline 88\end{array}$$

$$\begin{array}{r}674\\-235\\\hline 439\end{array}$$

$$\begin{array}{r}865\\-378\\\hline 487\end{array}$$

$$\begin{array}{r}347\\-158\\\hline 189\end{array}$$

$$\begin{array}{r}880\\-506\\\hline 374\end{array}$$

$$\begin{array}{r}432\\-243\\\hline 189\end{array}$$

$$\begin{array}{r}976\\-577\\\hline 399\end{array}$$

$$\begin{array}{r}764\\-198\\\hline 566\end{array}$$

$$\begin{array}{r}515\\-239\\\hline 276\end{array}$$

$$\begin{array}{r}831\\-743\\\hline 88\end{array}$$

$$\begin{array}{r}848\\-349\\\hline 499\end{array}$$

$$\begin{array}{r}652\\-378\\\hline 274\end{array}$$

$$\begin{array}{r}977\\-879\\\hline 98\end{array}$$

Addition and Subtraction

---

# Math Concentration

Add or subtract using regrouping.
Color the two cards with matching answers.

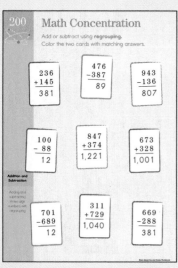

$$\begin{array}{r}236\\+145\\\hline 381\end{array}$$

$$\begin{array}{r}476\\-387\\\hline 89\end{array}$$

$$\begin{array}{r}943\\-136\\\hline 807\end{array}$$

$$\begin{array}{r}100\\-88\\\hline 12\end{array}$$

$$\begin{array}{r}847\\+374\\\hline 1,221\end{array}$$

$$\begin{array}{r}673\\+328\\\hline 1,001\end{array}$$

$$\begin{array}{r}701\\-689\\\hline 12\end{array}$$

$$\begin{array}{r}311\\+729\\\hline 1,040\end{array}$$

$$\begin{array}{r}669\\-288\\\hline 381\end{array}$$

Addition and Subtraction

---

# Times Fly

Finish the addition and multiplication sentences for each picture.

## Brain Box

$$2 + 2 + 2 + 2 = 8$$

$$2 \times 4 = 8$$

$$5 + 5 + 5 + 5 = 20$$

$$5 \times 4 = 20$$

$$3 + 3 + 3 + 3 + 3 = 15$$

$$3 \times 5 = 15$$

Multiplication and Fractions

$$4 + 4 + 4 = 12$$

$$4 \times 3 = 12$$

$$6 + 6 = 12$$

$$2 \times 6 = 12$$

Multiplication and Fractions

---

# Harvest Times

Finish the addition sentences.

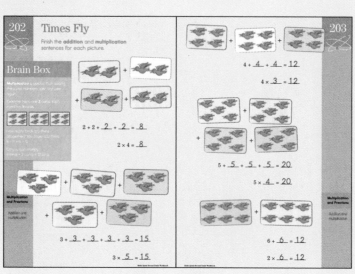

$$5 + 5 + 5 = 15$$

Another way to write this sentence is like this:

$$\begin{array}{r}5\\+\\5\\+\\5\\\hline 15\end{array}$$

$$15$$

Multiplication and Fractions

## Brain Box

Now write the same equation as a multiplication sentence.

$$5 \times 3 = 15$$

Can you write the multiplication sentence the other way?

$$\begin{array}{r}5\\\times 3\\\hline 15\end{array}$$

Rewrite the addition sentence as a multiplication sentence.

$$6 + 6 + 6 = 18$$

$$6 \times 3 = 18$$

$$\begin{array}{r}6\\\times 3\\\hline 18\end{array}$$

Multiplication and Fractions

---

# Balloons!

Solve each problem.
Find the multiplication balloon that matches the addition balloon. Color it the same color.

$$\begin{array}{r}8\\\times 4\\\hline 32\end{array}$$

$$6 + 6 + 6 + 6 = 24$$

$$\begin{array}{r}1\\\times 5\\\hline 5\end{array}$$

$$\begin{array}{r}8\\8\\8\\+8\\\hline 32\end{array}$$

$$\begin{array}{r}1\\1\\1\\1\\+1\\\hline 5\end{array}$$

$$\begin{array}{r}6\\\times 4\\\hline 24\end{array}$$

Multiplication and Fractions

# Time to Multiply

Multiply. Color each box yellow that equals less than 12.

| | | |
|---|---|---|
| $4 \times 4 = 16$ | $3 \times 2 = 6$ | $5 \times 4 = 20$ |
| $5 \times 5 = 25$ | $2 \times 2 = 4$ | $3 \times 5 = 15$ |
| $3 \times 3 = 9$ | $4 \times 1 = 4$ | $0 \times 5 = 0$ |
| $2 \times 1 = 2$ | $5 \times 2 = 10$ | $8 \times 1 = 8$ |
| $5 \times 3 = 15$ | $2 \times 0 = 0$ | $4 \times 5 = 20$ |
| $4 \times 3 = 12$ | $3 \times 3 = 9$ | $3 \times 5 = 15$ |

What math symbol did you color? _an addition sign_

What does the symbol tell you to do? _add_

Multiplication and Fractions

---

# Table Times 10

Write the missing numbers in the times table.

| × | 0 | 1 | 2 | 3 | 4 | 5 | 6 | 7 | 8 | 9 | 10 |
|---|---|---|---|---|---|---|---|---|---|---|---|
| 0 | 0 | 0 | 0 | 0 | 0 | 0 | 0 | 0 | 0 | 0 | 0 |
| 1 | 0 | 1 | 2 | 3 | 4 | 5 | 6 | 7 | 8 | 9 | 10 |
| 2 | 0 | 2 | 4 | 6 | 8 | 10 | 12 | 14 | 16 | 18 | 20 |
| 3 | 0 | 3 | 6 | 9 | 12 | 15 | 18 | 21 | 24 | 27 | 30 |
| 4 | 0 | 4 | 8 | 12 | 16 | 20 | 24 | 28 | 32 | 36 | 40 |
| 5 | 0 | 5 | 10 | 15 | 20 | 25 | 30 | 35 | 40 | 45 | 50 |
| 6 | 0 | 6 | 12 | 18 | 24 | 30 | 36 | 42 | 48 | 54 | 60 |
| 7 | 0 | 7 | 14 | 21 | 28 | 35 | 42 | 49 | 56 | 63 | 70 |
| 8 | 0 | 8 | 16 | 24 | 32 | 40 | 48 | 56 | 64 | 72 | 80 |
| 9 | 0 | 9 | 18 | 27 | 36 | 45 | 54 | 63 | 72 | 81 | 90 |
| 10 | 0 | 10 | 20 | 30 | 40 | 50 | 60 | 70 | 80 | 90 | 100 |

Multiplication and Fractions

## Brain Box

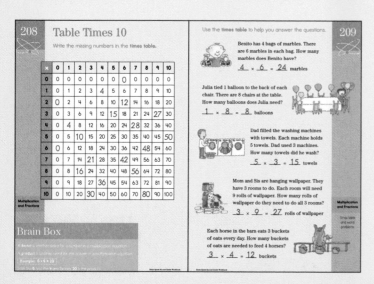

Use the times table to help you answer the questions.

Benito has 4 bags of marbles. There are 6 marbles in each bag. How many marbles does Benito have?

$$4 \times 6 = 24 \text{ marbles}$$

Julia tied 1 balloon to the back of each chair. There are 8 chairs at the table. How many balloons does Julia need?

$$1 \times 8 = 8 \text{ balloons}$$

Dad filled the washing machines with towels. Each machine holds 5 towels. Dad used 3 machines. How many towels did he wash?

$$5 \times 3 = 15 \text{ towels}$$

Mom and Sis are hanging wallpaper. They have 3 rooms to do. Each room will need 9 rolls of wallpaper. How many rolls of wallpaper do they need to do all 3 rooms?

$$3 \times 9 = 27 \text{ rolls of wallpaper}$$

Each horse in the barn eats 3 buckets of oats every day. How many buckets of oats are needed to feed 4 horses?

$$3 \times 4 = 12 \text{ buckets}$$

Multiplication and Fractions

---

# $\frac{1}{2}$ Equals One Half

Color one half of each shape.
Write the fraction in the space you colored.

$$\frac{1}{2}$$

$$\frac{1}{2}$$

$$\frac{1}{2}$$

$$\frac{1}{2}$$

Fractions

## Brain Box

# $\frac{1}{4}$ Equals One Quarter

Color one quarter of each shape.
Write the fraction in the space you colored.

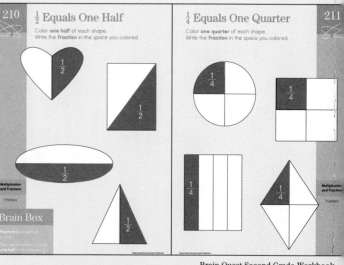

$$\frac{1}{4}$$

$$\frac{1}{4}$$

$$\frac{1}{4}$$

$$\frac{1}{4}$$

Multiplication and Fractions

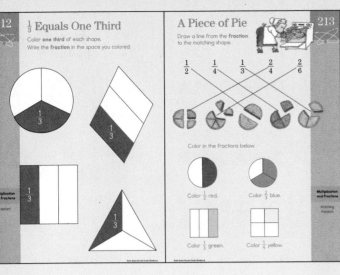

# ⅓ Equals One Third

Color **one third** of each shape.
Write the **fraction** in the space you colored.

⅓  ⅓  ⅓  ⅓

Multiplication and Fractions

## A Piece of Pie

Draw a line from the **fraction** to the matching shape.

½    ¼    ⅓    ²⁄₄    ²⁄₆

Color in the fractions below.

Color ½ red.    Color ⅔ blue.

Color ⅓ green.    Color ¼ yellow.

Multiplication and Fractions

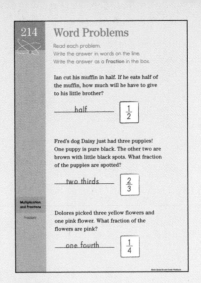

# Word Problems

Read each problem.
Write the answer in words on the line.
Write the answer as a **fraction** in the box.

Ian cut his muffin in half. If he eats half of the muffin, how much will he have to give to his little brother?

half    [ ½ ]

Fred's dog Daisy just had three puppies! One puppy is pure black. The other two are brown with little black spots. What fraction of the puppies are spotted?

two thirds    [ ⅔ ]

Dolores picked three yellow flowers and one pink flower. What fraction of the flowers are pink?

one fourth    [ ¼ ]

Multiplication and Fractions

Fractions

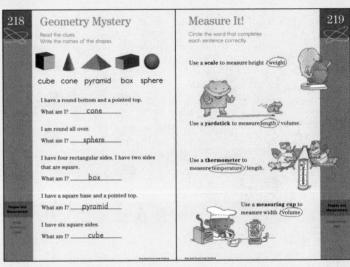

# Name That Shape!

Read the clues.
Write the names of the **shapes**.

○  □  ◇  ▭  △

I have four sides. Two of my sides are short. Two are long.
What am I?    rectangle

I have no sides at all. I go round and round.
What am I?    circle

I have four sides. Each side is the same.
What am I?    square

I have four sides. You can find me in a deck of cards or on a baseball field.
What am I?    diamond

I have three sides.
What am I?    triangle

Shapes and Measurement

## Same Shape

Look at the shape on the top card.
Draw a matching shape on the card below.

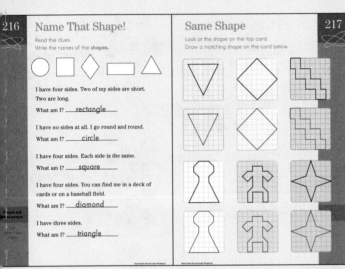

# Geometry Mystery

Read the clues.
Write the names of the shapes.

cube  cone  pyramid  box  sphere

I have a round bottom and a pointed top.
What am I?    cone

I am round all over.
What am I?    sphere

I have four rectangular sides. I have two sides that are square.
What am I?    box

I have a square base and a pointed top.
What am I?    pyramid

I have six square sides.
What am I?    cube

Shapes and Measurement

## Measure It!

Circle the word that completes each sentence correctly.

Use a **scale** to measure height /(weight).

Use a **yardstick** to measure (length)/ volume.

Use a **thermometer** to measure (temperature)/ length.

Use a **measuring cup** to measure width /(volume).

Shapes and Measurement

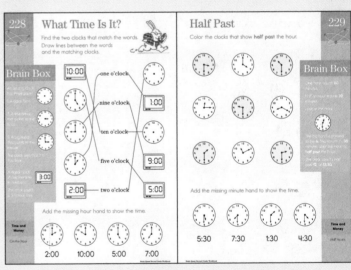

Write the **weight** of each basket of fruit.
Then answer the questions.

7 pounds    4 pounds

To measure the water in a swimming pool, would you use a cup or a gallon jug?
a gallon jug

To measure the distance from your room to the kitchen, would you use feet or miles?
feet

If the thermometer reads 35°F, would you wear a swimsuit or a snowsuit?
a snowsuit

Shapes and Measurement

## Inch by Inch

Cut out the **ruler** along the dotted line.
Use it to measure the pictures.
Then complete the sentences.
Save your ruler to use for the next five pages.

The quarter is 1 inch wide.

The teaspoon is 5 inches long.

The toy car is 3 inches long.

The key is 1½ inches long.

### Brain Box

Shapes and Measurement

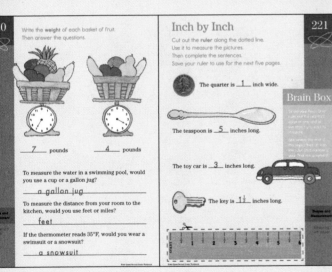

# What Time Is It?

Find the two clocks that match the words.
Draw lines between the words and the matching clocks.

Brain Box

one o'clock
nine o'clock
ten o'clock
five o'clock
two o'clock

Add the missing hour hand to show the time.

2:00    10:00    5:00    7:00

Time and Money

## Half Past

Color the clocks that show **half past** the hour.

### Brain Box

Add the missing minute hand to show the time.

5:30    7:30    1:30    4:30

Time and Money

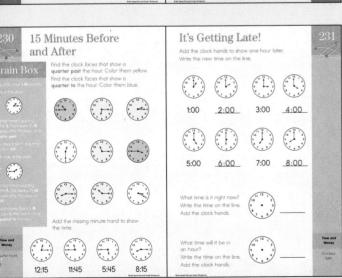

# 15 Minutes Before and After

### Brain Box

Find the clock faces that show a **quarter past** the hour. Color them yellow.
Find the clock faces that show a **quarter to** the hour. Color them blue.

Add the missing minute hand to show the time.

12:15    11:45    5:45    8:15

Time and Money

## It's Getting Late!

Add the clock hands to show one hour later.
Write the new time on the line.

1:00    2:00    3:00    4:00

5:00    6:00    7:00    8:00

What time is it right now?
Write the time on the line.
Add the clock hands.

What time will it be in an hour?
Write the time on the line.
Add the clock hands.

Time and Money

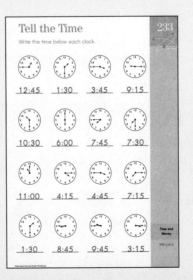

## Tell the Time

Write the time below each clock.

12:45    1:30    3:45    9:15

10:30    6:00    7:45    7:30

11:00    4:15    4:45    7:15

1:30    8:45    9:45    3:15

Time and Money

**Brain Quest Second Grade Workbook**

## Money Riddles

Read the clues and questions.
Circle the answers.

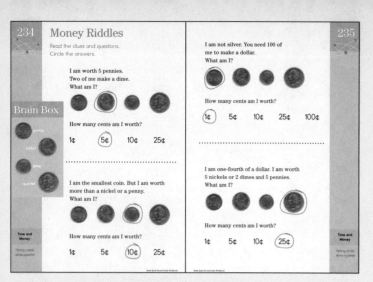

I am worth 5 pennies.
Two of me make a dime.
What am I?

How many cents am I worth?

1¢   (5¢)   10¢   25¢

### Brain Box

penny
nickel
dime
quarter

I am the smallest coin. But I am worth more than a nickel or a penny. What am I?

How many cents am I worth?

1¢   5¢   (10¢)   25¢

Time and Money

---

I am not silver. You need 100 of me to make a dollar. What am I?

How many cents am I worth?

(1¢)   5¢   10¢   25¢   100¢

I am one-fourth of a dollar. I am worth 5 nickels or 2 dimes and 5 pennies. What am I?

How many cents am I worth?

1¢   5¢   10¢   (25¢)

Time and Money

---

## Toy Store

Circle the exact change needed to buy each toy.
Then count the change left over.

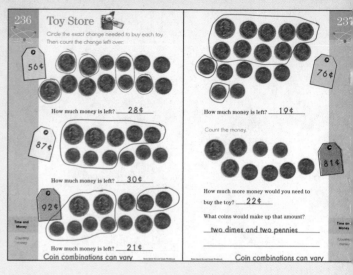

56¢   How much money is left? __28¢__

87¢   How much money is left? __30¢__

92¢   How much money is left? __21¢__

Time and Money

---

76¢   How much money is left? __19¢__

Count the money.

81¢

How much more money would you need to buy the toy? __22¢__

What coins would make up that amount?

__two dimes and two pennies__

Time and Money

**Coin combinations can vary**

---

## Got Change?

How many of each coin equal a **dollar**?
Write the missing numbers in the chart.

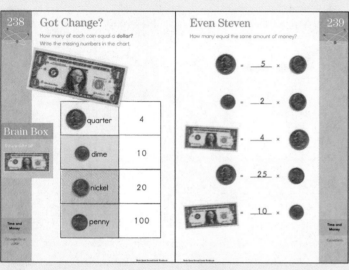

### Brain Box

| | |
|---|---|
| quarter | 4 |
| dime | 10 |
| nickel | 20 |
| penny | 100 |

Time and Money

---

## Even Steven

How many equal the same amount of money?

= __5__ × 

= __2__ × 

= __4__ × 

= __25__ × 

= __10__ × 

Time and Money

---

## Which Is More?

Add the coins.
Write the amount on the line.
Compare the coins to the dollar bill or bills.
Circle the **greater** amount.

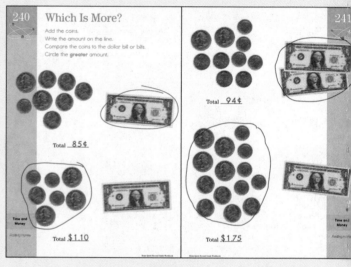

Total __85¢__

Total __$1.10__

---

Total __94¢__

Total __$1.75__

Time and Money

---

## Piggy Bank

Draw a line from each group of coins to the matching piggy bank.

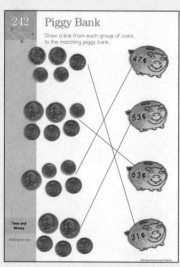

47¢
53¢
63¢
31¢

Time and Money

---

## State Capitals

Use the map that comes with this workbook to help you fill in the **state capitals**.

__Montgomery__ Alabama
__Juneau__ Alaska
__Phoenix__ Arizona
__Little Rock__ Arkansas
__Sacramento__ California
__Denver__ Colorado
__Hartford__ Connecticut
__Dover__ Delaware
__Tallahassee__ Florida
__Atlanta__ Georgia
__Honolulu__ Hawaii
__Boise__ Idaho
__Springfield__ Illinois

__Indianapolis__ Indiana
__Des Moines__ Iowa
__Topeka__ Kansas
__Frankfort__ Kentucky
__Baton Rouge__ Louisiana
__Augusta__ Maine
__Annapolis__ Maryland
__Boston__ Massachusetts
__Lansing__ Michigan
__St. Paul__ Minnesota
__Jackson__ Mississippi
__Jefferson City__ Missouri
__Helena__ Montana

Social Studies

---

__Lincoln__ Nebraska
__Carson City__ Nevada
__Concord__ New Hampshire
__Trenton__ New Jersey
__Santa Fe__ New Mexico
__Albany__ New York
__Raleigh__ North Carolina
__Bismarck__ North Dakota
__Columbus__ Ohio
__Oklahoma City__ Oklahoma
__Salem__ Oregon
__Harrisburg__ Pennsylvania

__Providence__ Rhode Island
__Columbia__ South Carolina
__Pierre__ South Dakota
__Nashville__ Tennessee
__Austin__ Texas
__Salt Lake City__ Utah
__Montpelier__ Vermont
__Richmond__ Virginia
__Olympia__ Washington
__Charleston__ West Virginia
__Madison__ Wisconsin
__Cheyenne__ Wyoming

What is the capital of the country?

__Washington, D.C.__

Social Studies

---

## Map It!

Use the **map key** to label the continents.

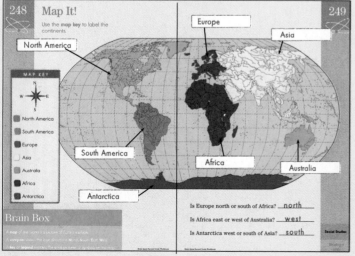

North America
South America
Europe
Asia
Africa
Australia
Antarctica

MAP KEY

- North America
- South America
- Europe
- Asia
- Australia
- Africa
- Antarctica

### Brain Box

---

Is Europe north or south of Africa? __north__

Is Africa east or west of Australia? __west__

Is Antarctica west or south of Asia? __south__

Social Studies

---

## Following Directions

Use the **map** on the next page to complete the sentences.
All the kids start at school.

I am going 4 blocks north and 1 block east.

Josh is going to the __music school__.

Jen is going to the __ball field__.

I am going 2 blocks south and 2 blocks west.

I am going 2 blocks south and 2 blocks east.

Jane is going to the __market__.

I am going 1 block north and 3 blocks east.

Jeremy is going to the __library__.

Social Studies

---

## Calendar Crunch

Write the months of the year in order on the **time line**.
Use the words in the box.

1 — January
2 — February
3 — March
4 — April
5 — May
6 — June
7 — July
8 — August
9 — September
10 — October
11 — November
12 — December

| |
|---|
| April |
| August |
| December |
| February |
| January |
| July |
| June |
| March |
| May |
| November |
| October |
| September |

Social Studies

**Brain Quest Second Grade Workbook**

## 257

Fill in the blanks on the **time line**.

| mail | telegraph | telephone | Pony Express | cell phone |

Long ago — 1840s — 1860s — Today

1900s

How do you think people will communicate in the future?
Describe and draw your "communication invention" of the future.

_____
_____
_____
_____

## 261

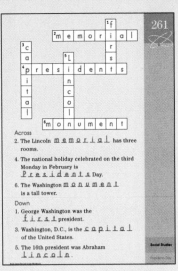

Crossword puzzle:

```
        ¹f
²m e m o r i a l
        r
³c   ⁵L  s
⁴p r e s i d e n t s
a   i   c
p   n   o
i   c   l
t   o   n
a   l
l
        ⁶m o n u m e n t
```

**Across**
2. The Lincoln **memorial** has three rooms.
4. The national holiday celebrated on the third Monday in February is **Presidents** Day.
6. The Washington **monument** is a tall tower.

**Down**
1. George Washington was the **first** president.
3. Washington, D.C., is the **capital** of the United States.
5. The 16th president was Abraham **Lincoln**.

Social Studies

## 262 Big Birthdays

Read about the Fourth of July.

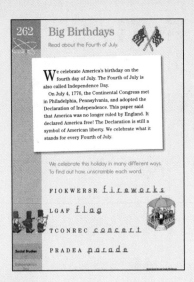

We celebrate America's birthday on the fourth day of July. The Fourth of July is also called Independence Day.

On July 4, 1776, the Continental Congress met in Philadelphia, Pennsylvania, and adopted the Declaration of Independence. This paper said that America was no longer ruled by England. It declared America free! The Declaration is still a symbol of American liberty. We celebrate what it stands for every Fourth of July.

We celebrate this holiday in many different ways. To find out how, unscramble each word.

FIOKWERSR **fireworks**

LGAF **flag**

TCONREC **concert**

PRADEA **parade**

Social Studies

## 264 American Women

Read about these important American women.
Write their names and birthdays on the **time line** below.

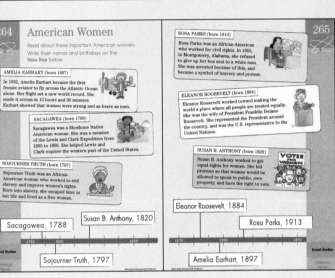

**AMELIA EARHART (born 1897)**
In 1932, Amelia Earhart became the first female aviator to fly across the Atlantic Ocean alone. Her flight set a new world record. She made it across in 13 hours and 30 minutes. Earhart showed that women were strong and as brave as men.

**SACAGAWEA (born 1788)**
Sacagawea was a Shoshone Native American woman. She was a member of the Lewis and Clark Expedition from 1805 to 1806. She helped Lewis and Clark explore the western part of the United States.

**SOJOURNER TRUTH (born 1797)**
Sojourner Truth was an African-American woman who worked to end slavery and improve women's rights. Born into slavery, she escaped later in her life and lived as a free woman.

Sacagawea, 1788 | Susan B. Anthony, 1820
Sojourner Truth, 1797

Social Studies

## 265

**ROSA PARKS (born 1913)**
Rosa Parks was an African-American who worked for civil rights. In 1955, in Montgomery, Alabama, she refused to give up her bus seat to a white man. She was arrested because of this, and became a symbol of bravery and protest.

**ELEANOR ROOSEVELT (born 1884)**
Eleanor Roosevelt worked toward making the world a place where all people are treated equally. She was the wife of President Franklin Delano Roosevelt. She represented the President around the country, and was the U.S. representative to the United Nations.

**SUSAN B. ANTHONY (born 1820)**
Susan B. Anthony worked to get equal rights for women. She led protests so that women would be allowed to speak in public, own property, and have the right to vote.

VOTES FOR WOMEN

Eleanor Roosevelt, 1884 | Rosa Parks, 1913
Amelia Earhart, 1897

## 266 American Men

Read about these important American men.
Write their names and birthdays on the **time line** below.

**PAUL REVERE (born 1735)**
Paul Revere was an important American patriot. He was an ordinary man who worked as a silversmith. But one night in 1775, he rode from Boston toward Concord, Massachusetts, to warn the Americans there that British troops were coming. This act of bravery helped America win her independence.

**THOMAS EDISON (born 1847)**
Thomas Edison was one of the greatest inventors of all time. He invented more than 1,000 different things, including the electric light and the movie camera. His inventions forever changed the way people work and play.

**THURGOOD MARSHALL (born 1908)**
Thurgood Marshall was the first African-American justice on the U.S. Supreme Court. He began his career as a civil rights lawyer. In 1954 he won a case called *Brown v. Board of Education*. This made segregation illegal, and paved the way for the civil rights movement in America.

Paul Revere, 1735
Thomas Edison, 1847

Social Studies

## 267

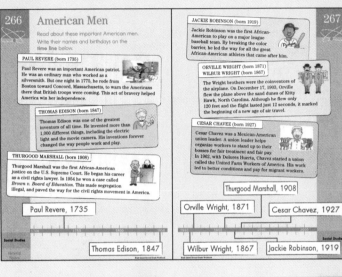

**JACKIE ROBINSON (born 1919)**
Jackie Robinson was the first African-American to play on a major league baseball team. By breaking the color barrier, he led the way for all the great African-American athletes that came after him.

**ORVILLE WRIGHT (born 1871)**
**WILBUR WRIGHT (born 1867)**
The Wright brothers were the coinventors of the airplane. On December 17, 1903, Orville flew the plane above the sand dunes of Kitty Hawk, North Carolina. Although he flew only 120 feet and the flight lasted just 12 seconds, it marked the beginning of a new age of air travel.

**CESAR CHAVEZ (born 1927)**
Cesar Chavez was a Mexican-American union leader. A union leader helps organize workers to stand up to their bosses for fair treatment and fair pay. In 1962, with Dolores Huerta, Chavez started a union called the United Farm Workers of America. His work led to better conditions and pay for migrant workers.

Thurgood Marshall, 1908
Orville Wright, 1871 | Cesar Chavez, 1927
Wilbur Wright, 1867 | Jackie Robinson, 1919

Social Studies

## 270 What Am I?

Read the riddles.
Answer each riddle with a word from the Word Box.

| gold | turtle |
| potato | coal |
| snail | carrot |

I grow underground.
French fries are made of me.
What am I? **potato**

I hatch from an egg, but I have no feathers. I carry my home with me. When I'm scared, I pull my head and four legs inside my shell.
What am I? **turtle**

### Brain Box
An animal is a living creature.
A vegetable is a food that people and animals can eat.
A mineral is found underground in the ground.

I'm found in rocks underground. I'm a shiny yellow color. I make a pretty ring or necklace.
What am I? **gold**

I'm orange. Rabbits find me very yummy!
What am I? **carrot**

Science

## 271

I travel very slowly inch by inch.
What am I? **snail**

I can be used for fuel.
What am I? **coal**

Write each word from the Word Box under the correct heading in the chart. Then add one of your own words to each column.

| Animals | Vegetables | Minerals |
|---------|-----------|----------|
| turtle | potato | gold |
| snail | carrot | coal |

Science

## 273

Label each picture with a phrase from the box.

| rain falls | clouds form |
| water vapor rises | sun shines |

sun shines

water vapor rises

clouds form

rain falls

The water cycle.

Science

## 275

Write **liquid**, **gas**, or **solid** under each picture.

solid | gas

liquid | gas

liquid | solid

Science

## 277

Read about the experiment.
Number the pictures to show the correct order of the steps.

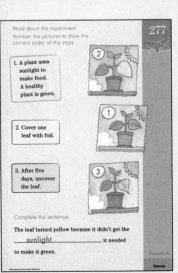

2
1
3

1. A plant uses sunlight to make food. A healthy plant is green.

2. Cover one leaf with foil.

3. After five days, uncover the leaf.

Complete the sentence.

The leaf turned yellow because it didn't get the **sunlight** it needed to make it green.

Science

## 278 Light

Read about **light**.

Is light white? No! Light is made up of colors. When light passes through raindrops, high above the earth, the light rays bend. When light bends, we see the colors of the rainbow.

R for red
O for orange
Y for yellow
G for green
B for blue
I for indigo
V for violet

What are the colors of the rainbow? You can remember the colors of the rainbow in order by remembering the name "ROY G. BIV." Red is usually on the outside part of the rainbow; violet is usually on the inside part.

Color the rainbow.

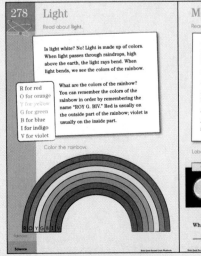

ROYGBIV

Science

## 279 Moonlight

Read about the **moon**.

The moon goes through phases as it travels around Earth. The shapes of the phases are the parts of the moon lit by the sun.

A full moon is round like a circle.

A half moon is half a circle.

A crescent moon looks like a sideways smile. It is smaller than a half moon.

A gibbous moon is smaller than a crescent moon.

A new moon is not visible because the side of the moon facing Earth gets no sunlight.

Label the phases of the moon.

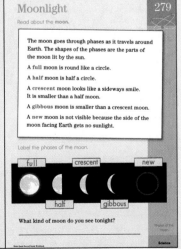

full | crescent | new
half | gibbous

What kind of moon do you see tonight?

_____

Science

Brain Quest Second Grade Workbook

Circle **Earth** in the picture below.
Use the picture to answer the questions.

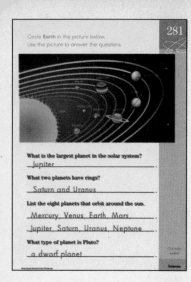

What is the largest planet in the solar system?
_Jupiter_

What two planets have rings?
_Saturn and Uranus_

List the eight planets that orbit around the sun.
_Mercury, Venus, Earth, Mars,_
_Jupiter, Saturn, Uranus, Neptune_

What type of planet is Pluto?
_a dwarf planet_

---

## Stay Healthy!

Maiko loves to jump rope to stay healthy.
She made a **chart** to keep track of how long she jumps rope each day.
Use her chart to answer the questions.

| CHART | |
|-------|---------|
| Day | Minutes |
| Mon. | 15 |
| Tues. | 10 |
| Wed. | 20 |
| Thurs. | 12 |
| Fri. | 18 |
| Sat. | 18 |
| Sun. | 13 |

On which day did Maiko exercise the most?
_Wednesday_

On which day did she exercise the least?
_Tuesday_

On which two days did she exercise the same amount of time?
_Friday and Saturday_

Use the **chart** to complete the **graph** for Thursday through Sunday.

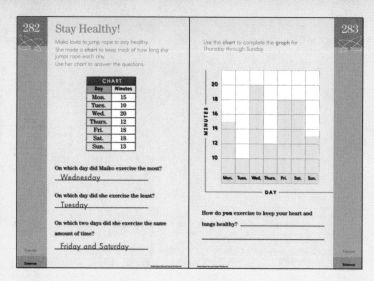

How do **you** exercise to keep your heart and lungs healthy? _____

---

| Kenya |
|-------|
| oceans |
| fable |
| rough |
| years |

Use words from the Word Box to complete the sentences.

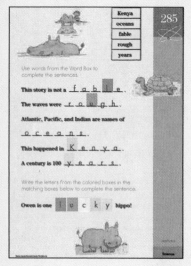

This story is not a  f a b l e .

The waves were  r o u g h .

Atlantic, Pacific, and Indian are names of
o c e a n s .

This happened in  K e n y a .

A century is 100  y e a r s .

Write the letters from the colored boxes in the matching boxes below to complete the sentence.

Owen is one  l u c k y  hippo!

---

## Bird Riddles

Draw a line from each bird riddle on this page to the correct bird on the next page.

My tail is so beautiful! I can fly, but I would rather walk and strut. What am I?

I have feathers and a beak, and I lay eggs like other birds. But I do not fly through the air. I fly through the water! What am I?

I am a beautiful bird, too! I have a sharp beak. If you are patient, you might be able to teach me to say, "Polly want a cracker." What am I?

I am tall. I have a long neck. My feathers are pink from the pink shrimp I like to eat. What am I?

I am a small bird. The feathers on my chest are red. You see me in the spring. What am I?

I have a red comb on top of my head. In the early morning you might hear me call, "cock-a-doodle-do!" What am I?

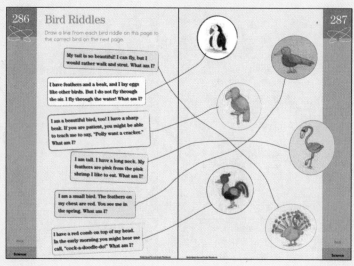

---

Match the words on the frog with the definitions on the lily pads.

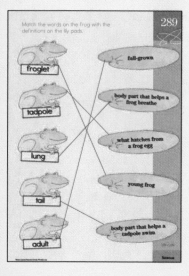

froglet

tadpole

lung

tail

adult

full-grown

body part that helps a frog breathe

what hatches from a frog egg

young frog

body part that helps a tadpole swim

---

## The Camel's a Mammal

Read about **mammals**.

**All Mammals:**
✓ breathe air through lungs.
✓ are born alive. They do not hatch.
✓ drink milk their mothers make.
✓ have hair. Some are born with hair and lose it as they grow up.

Circle all the mammals.

Most mammals live on land, but some mammals live in the sea.

Sea mammals have lungs. They swim up to the surface to breathe air.

Sea creatures that are not mammals do not need to breathe air.

Circle the sea creatures that are mammals.

# Brain Quest
# Extras

# Congratulations!

You've finished the Brain Quest Workbook!

In this section, you'll find:

## Brain Quest Mini-Deck

Cut out the cards and make your own Brain Quest deck.

Play by yourself or with a friend.

## Brainiac Certificate

Put a sticker on each square for every chapter you complete. Finish the whole workbook, and you're an official Brainiac!

And don't forget to turn to the end of the workbook. You'll find stickers and a United States map!

## Questions

How many hundreds are in the number 839?

What's a shorter way to say "I am"?

Which is more: 4 pennies + 4 nickels, or 2 dimes?

Find the verb in this sentence: "The red ball flew through the air."

## Questions

Find the sum: 60 + 67.

If "d" and "r" are called consonants, what are "a" and "i" called?

My sister is 15 years old. How old will she be in 6 years?

How many beds does Goldilocks try?

## Questions

Ariel drew a picture of 6 trees. Then she drew 3 flowers. How many plants did she draw in all?

Synonyms are words that have opposite meanings. True or false?

Which number doesn't belong here: 3, 7, 4, 9, 11?

Which word begins with an "s" sound: crispy, caterpillar, cereal, court?

## Questions

Is the sum of 46 + 52 more or less than 100?

To find out the meaning of a word, do you use an atlas or a dictionary?

What do we call the total when three numbers are added together?

Which is the correct spelling for a birthday dessert: c-a-k-e or c-a-c-k-e?

## Questions

Pranith has four dimes, three nickels, and one penny. How much money does he have in all?

Find two synonyms: sad, polite, considerate, smiling.

Aurelia had 6 peaches. She gave 2 to her sister. How many peaches did Aurelia have left?

What's a longer way to say "haven't"?

## Questions

Double 16. What number do you get?

Which spelling has an extra "r": f-u-r-r-y, v-e-r-r-y, or h-u-r-r-y?

It's 7:30 a.m. What time will it be in 30 minutes?

How many dimes add up to 60¢?

## Answers

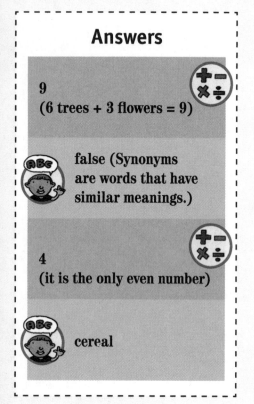

9
(6 trees + 3 flowers = 9)

false (Synonyms are words that have similar meanings.)

4
(it is the only even number)

cereal

## Answers

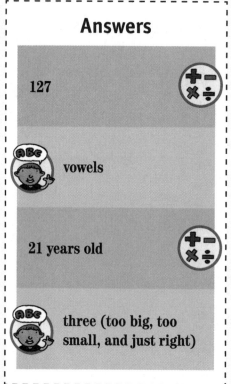

127

vowels

21 years old

three (too big, too small, and just right)

## Answers

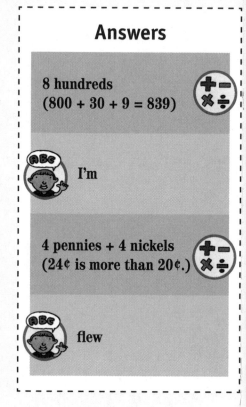

8 hundreds
(800 + 30 + 9 = 839)

I'm

4 pennies + 4 nickels
(24¢ is more than 20¢.)

flew

## Answers

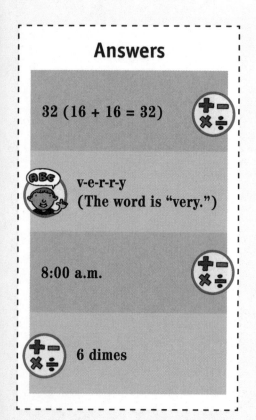

32 (16 + 16 = 32)

v-e-r-r-y
(The word is "very.")

8:00 a.m.

6 dimes

## Answers

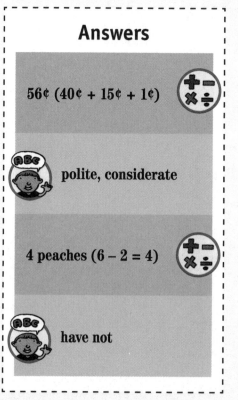

56¢ (40¢ + 15¢ + 1¢)

polite, considerate

4 peaches (6 − 2 = 4)

have not

## Answers

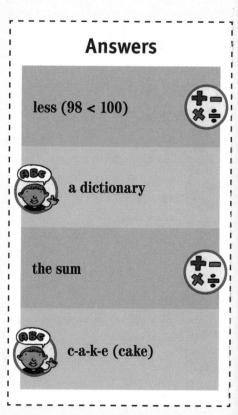

less (98 < 100)

a dictionary

the sum

c-a-k-e (cake)

## Questions

Fernando wants 15 postcards to mail to his friends. He has 6. How many more does he need?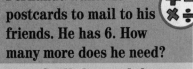

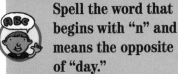 Spell the word that begins with "n" and means the opposite of "day."

I bought paints for $3 and a brush for $1.50. How much did I spend?

 What word can you put in front of "bug" to name a red insect with black spots?

## Questions

Find the difference: 47 – 13.

 To learn about current events, should you look in a newspaper or an encyclopedia?

How many nickels add up to 40¢?

 Correct this sentence: "She ain't coming to dinner."

## Questions

Is the number 2 worth more in 325 or 582?

 Which spelling is correct: n-i-c-k-e-l or n-i-c-k-l-e?

Find the difference: 37 – 5

 Find two words with the opposite meaning: blue, dark, light, pale.

## Questions

It's 9 o'clock in the morning. What time will it be in 5 hours?

 Which spelling needs a "k" at the beginning to make a word: n-o-r-t-h or n-i-f-e?

How much is 58 – 9?

 Rearrange the letters in the word "span" to make a word that means "more than one pot."

## Questions

Which looks more like a circle: a quarter or a dollar bill?

 What word is "hippo" short for?

What's the math term for 5 in this problem: 6 – 1 = 5?

 If a boy can be a brother, what can a girl be?

## Questions

Mia had two dozen cookies. She ate five of them. How many did she have left?

Is the word for a warm drink spelled t-e-a or t-e-e?

How much is 5 + 5 + 8?

Put these words in alphabetical order: duck, pig, horse, cow.

## Answers

325 (where the number 2 stands for 20)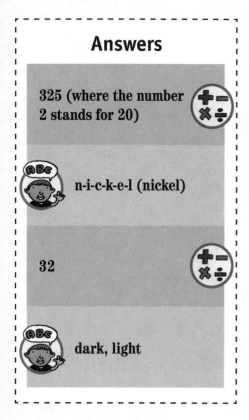

n-i-c-k-e-l (nickel)

32

dark, light

## Answers

34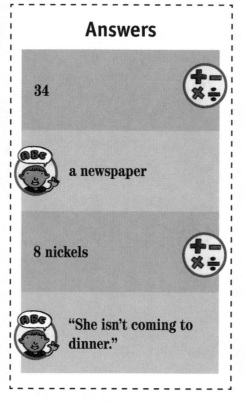

a newspaper

8 nickels

"She isn't coming to dinner."

## Answers

9 (15 – 6 = 9)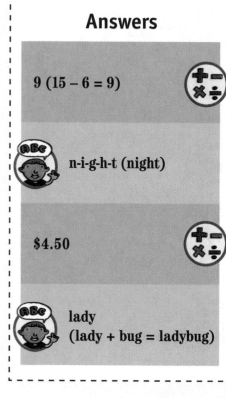

n-i-g-h-t (night)

$4.50

lady (lady + bug = ladybug)

## Answers

19 (24 – 5 = 19)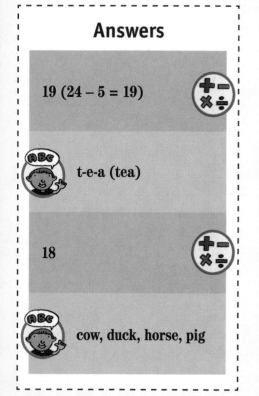

t-e-a (tea)

18

cow, duck, horse, pig

## Answers

a quarter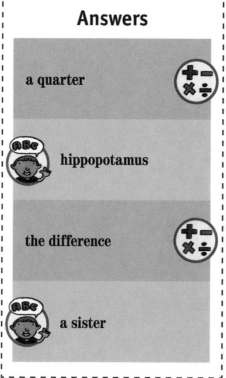

hippopotamus

the difference

a sister

## Answers

2 o'clock (2:00)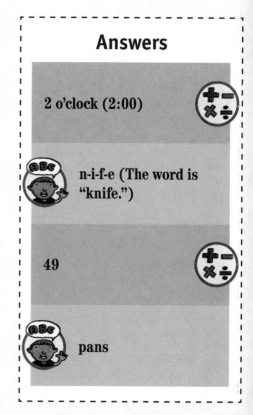

n-i-f-e (The word is "knife.")

49

pans

## Questions

How many wheels does a tricycle have?

 Who wants to blow down the houses of the Three Little Pigs?

How much is 68 + 7?

 Which should be written as one word: sand box or sand dune?

## Questions

If 4 + 3 equals 7, what does 4 + 3 + 3 equal?

 What two letters must you put before "a-g-o-n" to spell the name of a fire-breathing creature?

Which doesn't measure length: an inch, a pound, or a centimeter?

 The subject is one part of a sentence. What do we call the other part?

## Questions

How many tens and ones do you need to make 88?

 Put these words in alphabetical order: seven, cup, book, mouth

What time is it when the little hand is on the 3 and the big hand is on the 2?

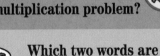 What's the word for more than one mouse?

## Questions

Ben needs 35 marbles. He has 18 blue ones and 15 green ones. Does he have enough?

 Which word comes first in a dictionary: mouse or giraffe?

Which is greater: the age of a second grader or the number of legs on a cat?

 Which word is NOT a verb: grow, sit, child?

## Questions

Suki has 10 oranges. She gives 7 to her cousin. How many does she have left?

 Rearrange the letters in the word "dam" to make another word for "angry."

Which set of numbers does NOT add up to 12: 6 + 2 + 4 or 3 + 7 + 5?

 Correct this sentence: "Noah lent paper to Roberto and I."

## Questions

How do you write 5 + 5 + 5 as a multiplication problem?

Which two words are antonyms: small, slow, heavy, large?

Find the shape of a postcard: circle, oval, rectangle.

Correct this sentence: "This is the most nice shirt I own."

## Answers

8 tens and 8 ones

book, cup, mouth, seven

3:10

mice

## Answers

10 (or 3 more)

d-r (dragon)

a pound

the predicate

## Answers

3 (tri- means "three.")

the Big Bad Wolf

75

sandbox

## Answers

5 × 3

large, small

rectangle

"This is the nicest shirt I own."

## Answers

3 (10 − 7 = 3)

mad

3 + 7 + 5 (equals 15)

"Noah lent paper to Roberto and me."

## Answers

no (18 + 15 = 33)

giraffe

the age of a second grader (A cat has 4 legs.)

child

## Questions

April is 9 years old. Alex is twice her age. How old is Alex?

Correct this sentence: "Chris and me went to the beach."

How many tens are in the number 250?

Find the subject of this sentence: "Gabriela is very smart."

## Questions

What are the next two numbers in this pattern: 0, 3, 6, ___, ___?

Find the opposite of "fast": light, low, slow, still.

What is the sum of 17 + 21?

Is a blanket that can go on your bed called a quit or a quilt?

## Questions

A decade is 10 years. How many years are in 4 decades?

Which word is both a noun and a verb: duck or door?

My cousin will be 25 in 3 years. How old is he now?

Find the antonyms in this group: up, high, down, tall.

## Questions

How much is 834 – 100?

Which is correct: "Abdul is taller than Josie" or "Abdul is more taller than Josie"?

What is the sum of 24 + 13?

What letter is missing from this synonym of "tiniest": s-m-a-l-e-s-t

## Questions

What is the largest three-digit number you can make with these digits: 4, 9, 7?

Spell the word for the coin that's worth 10¢.

On a clock, how many minutes go by between the numbers 3 and 6?

Find the opposite of "asleep": bed, awake, tired, dream.

## Questions

4 + 9 = 7 + 6. True or false?

Turn this sentence into a question: "Suri is coming over."

Lee spent 2 dollars on a card and 4 dollars on ribbons. How much did she spend in all?

What do we call two words that sound the same?

Brain Quest Second Grade Workbook

## Answers

40 years.

duck

22

up, down

---

## Answers

9, 12 (add 3)

slow

38

a quilt

---

## Answers

18 (9 + 9 = 18)

"Chris and I went to the beach."

5

Gabriela

---

## Answers

true (4 + 9 = 13; 7 + 6 = 13)

"Is Suri coming over?"

6 dollars ($6)

homophones

---

## Answers

974

d-i-m-e (dime)

15 minutes

awake

---

## Answers

734

"Abdul is taller than Josie."

37

1 (The word is "smallest.")